WHAT HOME EDUCATORS AROUND THE COUNTRY ARE SAYING ABOUT *THE SOCIALIZATION TRAP*:

"You have done a great service to the home schooling community by writing... *The Socialization Trap* is a very valuable resource and I have already recommended it to members of my support group... I have also suggested your seminar to our state association... There are so many families that would benefit..." **Indiana**

"My mother-in-law was dead set against our home schooling. Then I gave her *The Socialization Trap* to read. A few days later she gave it back and said, 'This answered all my questions. By all means, teach the children at home.'" **Maryland**

"Thank you very much. I have a copy of *The Socialization Trap* which I wholeheartedly agree with." **Connecticut**

"We just read *The Socialization Trap* and were so affirmed in what we knew was the right way." **Oregon**

"We have enjoyed your book, *The Socialization Trap*— GREAT... Your book and example BUILD US UP!!!" **Hawaii**

The
Socialization
Trap

Avoiding the pitfalls of
age segregation

By Rick Boyer

The Socialization Trap
©1993, 1995 by Rick and Marilyn Boyer
Cover design by Christina Loh Boyer
ISBN 0-9708770-0-5

Published by The Learning Parent
2430 Sunnymeade Road
Rustburg, VA 24588
www.thelearningparent.com

The Learning Parent is dedicated to equipping and encouraging home school families to raise their children in the nurture and admonition of the Lord. "That the generation to come might know, even the children yet to be born, that they may arise and tell them to their children, that they should put their confidence in God, and not forget the works of God, but keep His command- ments."
Psalm 78:6-7

Printed in the United States of America.

ACKNOWLEDGEMENTS

Special thanks are due to a number of people for their contributions to this book:

My wife Marilyn has taught me more than anyone else about Christian parenting. She is the only home education expert I have ever met and her price is far above rubies.

My long-time friend, Wally Saunders spent a number of hours serving as my computer guru, a job requiring considerable skill and remarkable patience. You're a genius, Wally.

Rick and Debbie Carpenter contributed their time and talents on the cover in more ways than one.

Tracy Cooter handled the cover photo. He and his family have been real friends.

CONTENTS

INTRODUCTION

If you're a home educator, you have probably been challenged on the subject of social learning. If you're considering home education, you soon will be. It's commonly assumed that home taught children are at a disadvantage because they spend more time at home with their families than do other children, causing many parents to look for special "social occasions" outside the home and the normal family routine to expose their children to "kids their own age."

This is the Socialization Trap. Most home educators are ensnared in it because they simply don't realize that conventional wisdom pertaining to socialization is wrong. Age peer social groups are not helpful but harmful to children. The natural and Biblical pattern of family–based, age–integrated social development is the great need of the home education movement today. It is not in the artificial, pressure–cooker atmospere of the school that normal social learning is done, but in the home, the church, the community, the workplace. As moms and dads learn not to thrust their children out into the unguided, random social circle of age peer grouping but rather take them by the hand and lead them through the real world, they help them to escape the Trap and become healthy, capable social beings.

The material in this book is based on my understanding of Scriptural principles, the research of social scientists and our own family's experience in home education. In addition, the experience of numbers of other home teaching families has contributed to our understanding of the subject and it is for them and others like them this book was written. May it and they be used to glorify our God.

PART I: THE TRAP

Chapter 1

Blind Guides

This book is both a cry from the heart and an answer to cries from other hearts. Since Marilyn and I decided thirteen years ago not to send our oldest son to kindergarten and shortly thereafter not to send our children to school at all, we have seen the home education movement grow from a tiny seed to a great tree. Because we were among the first in our part of the country to teach at home and because our family grew to a rather...er, noticeable size, we have attracted a certain amount of attention and eventually found ourselves in a position of counselors to other moms and dads who wanted to do the same for their children as we were trying to do for ours. Our search for answers to our questions and those of our friends led to the development of the Learning Parent home education seminar, now a nine-hour presentation. It's been interesting to note that parents share common concerns and therefore, ask common questions.

In the early days, the first question most parents asked involved the issue of legality. Recent years have brought so much new legislation in response to the phenomenal growth of home education nationwide that nearly all of the fifty states make some legal provision for parents to teach at home. So now the number two question has moved into first place: Am I qualified to teach my children? Again, the widespread growth of the movement has made this issue less threatening as well. In some parts of the country it seems everybody's doing it. Most folks considering home education know someone who is doing it and appears no smarter than themselves. The question we heard perhaps third in order of frequency is the challenge that brought this book into existence: How will my child learn to get along with other people?

The socialization question now competes with competency to teach as the most common concern of new and prospective home educators. It is definitely the most common objection raised by detractors: "Oh, you're home schooling. Aren't you concerned about how all that isolation will affect your kids?" Translated, this means they assume home education is roughly equivalent to chaining the child to the basement wall and feeding him bones and bread crusts.

I don't see this question gradually resolving itself as have the other two. Or maybe it would be more accurate to say that it is getting resolved but in a sad and dangerous way. The question is being answered but the answer is wrong.

To understand the wrong answer, let's expand the question. When someone asks, "How will these kids learn to get along with others?" they mean, "How will these kids learn to get along with others if they don't grow up in school and the attendant age peer social structure?" Nine out of ten home educators and nearly everyone outside the movement would answer wrongly. They would say that home taught kids can compensate for the lack of peer exposure by being involved in youth activities in the church and neighborhood. They would say that the home teaching parent can (and presumably should) replace school socialization with a like product of a different brand. This answer is wrong and we believe it reflects a widely accepted myth which is killing the joy of home education for thousands of families. The purpose of this book is to show why this answer is wrong and that God has a better way.

THE MYTH

One of the great myths of our day is that the way modern America socializes its children is good and in fact the best way in which social skills and values can be learned. It assumes that peer groups are healthy for children and that this is why children are grouped by age in school. It assumes that children need lots of peer exposure and so extra activities are needed to bring children of the same age together even beyond school. To rephrase it, the great myth says that children need to spend large amounts of time with children their own age to learn to relate properly to other people.

The great myth can be seen as a compilation of related myths. Or we can compare it to an octopus and list these "tentacles" among others:

1. School is a great place to learn social skills.

2. Constant comparison and competitition are not harmful to children.

3. Team sports are the ideal way to learn teamwork, self-control and dedication to a goal.

4. Home educated children need special activities to compensate for their lack of social exposure.

5. Church activities should be age graded.

6. Dating teaches young people relationship skills they will need in marriage.

7. Television is a valuable socializer because it exposes children to the world outside their own home.

8. Social contacts should be made at random so that children will meet a wide spectrum of personality and character types.

I believe that each of these assumptions is wrong. That they form the bedrock of contemporary public opinion about child social development is irrelevant. Practically everybody believes them, but practically everybody believes man descended from monkeys, too. There was a time when common knowledge had it that the earth was flat. As General Sherman said, "Vox populi, vox humbug." That's Latin (mostly) and worth looking up.

The thing that bothers me is the fact that not only the secularist and the schoolist believe these things, but most Christian home educators as well. I'm not familiar with any surveys on this, but my experience indicates that a very high percentage of home educators kept or brought their kids home from school for social reasons. The peer group was *hurting* their children, so they took them out of it. Yet, most home educators turn right around and look for all sorts of age peer activities to put their children in, thereby creating the same type of situation that was hurting them before. They have acted properly on their protective instincts by deciding to teach at home but their own socialized thinking assumes that their children are now lacking something. So the children are soon in scouts, little league and several different church youth activities. It seems tragic to me that most home educators are not home enough to educate.

TWO MODELS AND THE ROAD BACK TO EGYPT

Why do so many people fall into this trap? It's because they have an unscriptural view of both socialization and the family. They assume that normal living—home, community, church, marketplace—does not provide enough opportunity for social development. Therefore, home education needs help in the form of contrived activities.

The problem is one of models. It never seems to occur to most people that Scripture might contain a plan for growing up and that learning how to deal with others might be a part of that plan. For that reason, we are left adrift on the tide of impulse and reaction for our ideas. Usually, we end up doing things as we have always seen them done. When we do, we have chosen contemporary society rather than Scripture for our model.

We generally choose between the two models of school and Scripture for our educational plan. Some few choose a retired and secluded lifestyle by isolating their family from society on a homestead in the Rockies, but most home educators stay where they are geographically and adjust their lifestyles. Researchers tell us that those phenomena which we observe frequently come to be accepted as normal. This is where we get the school model for education and why most of us accept it without searching the Scriptures to see whether God has a better way.

The school model for education includes a strong emphasis on peer group socialization. School children in America spend between thirty and forty hours per week with their age peers in large groups and the "well-rounded" ones more than that through extra-curricular activities. This has been common practice for decades and we are now conditioned to think of it as normal. Kids need lots of time with kids their own age. We don't know just why, but we assume it's so. After all, that's the way the government school professionals do it and the government would never deceive us, would they?

The tendency to use our contemporary society, with its school-dominated program for childhood as our model for home education produces some bizarre results. Moms who should be home reading to their babies are instead putting miles of their cars faster than Richard Petty. She's here, she's there, she's everywhere, carting her kids to this activity, that club, the other lesson—instead of being a "keeper at home," "her feet abide not in her house." Mom is exhausted, the kids are hyperactive and the baby hasn't been rocked. Whenever a mom gets a neat idea for a field trip she calls up a leader in the support group and there results what has been called a 'cattle drive' field trip. The drovers are obligated to be polite to each other, the mavericks distract each other and the museum director has long since retreated to his office closet where he now lies whimpering on the floor in fetal position. So why don't we arrange field trips for just our family? Because they're always done in large groups in school. And school is our model.

The school model leads parents into a thousand other indiscretions. Weekly tests, voluminous record keeping, term papers and a cornucopia of other schoolish characteristics adorn our otherwise sensible daily routines. But we're dealing with social learning here so you'll have to wait until another book to hear me rave about all that.

GROUP THERAPY

As I said before, the majority of home educators are off base concerning their children's social needs. In some cases all that is needed is time and reflection. It's a pretty big step for most people to make the decision to home educate at all and the socialization aspects of the equation usually have to take a back seat to the resolution of legal questions, acquiring curriculum materials, etc. Many a mom who starts out with an activity-equals-productivity attitude eventually comes to see the error of her ways and stops trying to make a school of herself.

But often a problem arises when parents try to develop a right home and learning life, because they are short on support and long on critics. Other people don't seem to understand that children (not to mention parents) need time at home to read, work, play, dream and just be themselves. They are indoctrinated with the schoolish assumption that in order to be a well-rounded person, a child should be involved in a plethora of activities outside the home.

Certainly, home education support groups deserve a share of the blame. Many times, and perhaps most of the time when couples feel a need to form such groups, they sense the need but don't clearly understand what it is they're searching for. What they really need is encouragement, sympathy and sharing of ideas among parents. Parent education and encouragement is the name of the game. But schoolism is imbedded so deeply in the average subconscious mind that support groups for parents usually turn into activity groups for children or families. And here we go again. A group that has formed to help home educators begins to keep educators away from home. Ideas for parent education programs begin to run shy and suddenly someone gets struck with a bolt of inspiration: "Hey, next month let's get together and take the kids to the zoo!"

No, let's not. If we have run out of things to do in these meetings, then let's cancel next month's meeting and each of us take our own kids to the zoo. Let's not take a mob there so that if one child is cranky, his emotional dyspepsia won't be a black eye for our whole group and the home education movement in general. Let's each have the privacy, time and concentration to answer our children's questions about the animals and enjoy with them their wonder and excitement. Let's sit with just our own kids on a park bench and enjoy some sunshine and cotton candy. Let's have a fun and enlightening trip to the zoo without the necessity of being polite to other adults and worrying about everybody else's children trying to join the polar bears for a swim.

Support groups can be very resourceful. Some even form youth groups to further separate children from parents and siblings. It's not all that uncommon to find one local group that offers 4-H, musical groups, different sorts of lessons and even sports teams. In short, a quasi-school system.

The Socialization Trap

This approach to home education reflects what I call the Road Back to Egypt phenomenon. Remember in Exodus where the Israelites had escaped slavery in Egypt but found that life on the road was without some of the amenities of the old lifestyle? Numbers Chapter 11 tells the story. The Israelites came to Moses complaining (not for the first time) that the traveling fare did not suit their cultivated appetites. They longed for the fleshpots of Egypt where they used to eat (am I reading this correctly?) cucumbers and melons, leeks and onions and garlic?! God had given these people a divinely appointed diet of manna, specially prepared and delivered by Gabriel's catering service and they were crying to return to Egypt and dwell together amidst two million cases of halitosis.

Thus be it ever. We just don't seem to know what's good for us. We spend our youth developing a taste for the junk food of the world system and when we have a chance to escape to health and freedom we can't kick the habit. We keep looking for the turnoff for the road back to Egypt.

This reminds me of a news story I read about a stable fire on some big Thoroughbred farm in Kentucky. The writer noted that the horses had to be led out of the barn and restrained to keep them from running back into the burning structure. They were so used to thinking of their stalls as their hideaway that when danger threatened they tried to run back inside after having been rescued.

A third allegory that comes to mind involves my grandfather's fox dogs. In my native Ozarks, fox hunting used to be a popular sport. A great uncle of mine said that when he died, he wanted a pipe sunk in the ground at the head of his grave so he could hear his fox hounds run. This fox hunting wasn't the tally-ho English type where rich guys in very questionable attire ride beautiful horses behind a pack of about a thousand yelping hounds. The old hillbillies would park the pickup truck out in the woods at night and turn their dogs loose to find and follow a fox's trail. Their excitement came from following the race by the sound of the dogs' baying, which told the men whose dog was in the lead, which first figured out a trick the fox had left in the trail, etc. This was big thrills in those days (I guess you'd have to have been there). As a kid, I went with Grandad but I generally spent the time bored and sleepy. I had more fun picking ticks off the dogs the next day.

Anyway, Grandad once bought a couple of new dogs whose behavior was rather strange. One of the first mornings they were on the place, he went to get them out of the barn and give them some sunshine. His habit was to chain them to cinder blocks out in the barnyard where they could enjoy the fresh air but couldn't escape to go hunting in the hot daylight hours. But these new dogs were afraid to leave the barn. When Grandad led them out, he had to drag them as they fought and whined, trying to get back inside. He explained that they were "barn dogs." The previous owner must have kept them in a barn or shed whenever they weren't hunting. They needed the sunlight and fresh air, but because it was unfamiliar they found it threatening. They struggled to retreat to their dark, smelly den in the barn.

I may be working allegories to death, but this Road Back to Egypt syndrome is the greatest obstacle to success in home education. We can't discuss social development and not deal with it. Countless couples have tried home education for a year or two and then gotten so disheartened with problems they created for themselves that they burned out and put their children back in school. Back they went to Egypt without realizing that the Promised Land was just a little farther along the road.

How do parents turn back to Egypt? By inadvertently recreating outside of school the same type of pressures the children faced in school. Running in circles to involve the children in a hundred activities with KIDS THEIR OWN AGE. Becoming taxi drivers and shelling out for unneeded lessons and social outings when what their children really need is plenty of time doing things with Mom and Dad, playing with, caring for and learning from older and younger siblings. We act as if any place in the world is better for children than their own homes when just the opposite is true.

BODY PAINS

The twentieth-century church deserves a share of the blame for the problems we're discussing. The church should be an encouragement to families but too often the two seem to be at cross purposes. Scripture makes clear that families are important to the church as the church is important to families. In fact, God places so much importance on the family that success in family responsibility is a requirement for church leaders (see I Tim. 3:4-6, Tit. 1:6).

Today's churches by and large, however, have failed the families they serve. Requirements for leaders have been relaxed so that it is no longer necessary for a man to have an exemplary relationship with his wife and children in order to attain a leadership role. Further, churches are not teaching parents to be successful spouses and parents. Sermons go forth on almost every conceivable topic, but messages that teach parents how to fulfill these critical roles are few and far between.

Perhaps the most damaging thing the modern church has done is the dividing of families. In our seminar I make the point that the age grading of children in schools prepares them only for a world that doesn't exist. That is, despite all the hype about learning to get along with others their own age, people in the real world need to deal with persons of *all* ages. When the new employee arrives for the first day on the job, he isn't told to report to plant B because that's where all the twenty-seven-year-olds work. When I joined the rescue squad years ago, I wasn't assigned to be on call the same night as the other guys in my age group. The neighborhoods in which we live may tend to attract retirees or yuppies one more than the other, but generally they contain a mix of ages. The real world is an age-integrated place. The only major social institution that has followed the school system in segregating people by age is the church.

The Pilgrims used to sit on log benches with babies on their laps through two-hour sermons (I'm not endorsing that time frame) and some churches today operate in a similar manner. We have a conservative Mennonite church near our home in which the parents with babies and toddlers sit in the back few rows and take their children out if they grow too restive and noisy. The nursery consists of a couple of rooms in the back where mothers can change or feed Baby or put him down in a bed if he goes to sleep. I'd like to see a church auditorium include a nursing mothers' room at the rear of the sanctuary with soundproof walls, one-way glass, rocking chairs, cribs, changing tables and space for toddlers who can't yet tolerate a whole service. Speakers could bring the service in but baby racket couldn't get out. Mothers could enjoy the service without leaving the baby in the nursery to be cared for by strangers and share germs through pacifiers and teething toys. Few churches today consider mothers and babies important enough to go to the additional expense of this facility, but maybe the time is coming. Anyway, somebody needed to suggest it.

The Socialization Trap

For now, it would be nice if moms didn't feel like Martians in the service at every peep from a little one. I know it's distracting when an infant yells, but let's be reasonable. Most parents are considerate enough to remove a child before he demolishes the spirit of the service with his wailing, and others can be discreetly coached. Where are the older women who should be offering to take a baby out so the burdened young mother can enjoy a whole service for a change? As a matter of fact, it's partly our own fault that we find a child's noises so distracting. It is we adults who are responsible for the fact that we're not used to kids in the service. At the risk of meddling just a bit: if we weren't so television intoxicated our powers of concentration could withstand a little more distraction.

There is a tremendous amount of pressure on families to divide and participate in church programs. In more active churches, there are age-segregated ministries for every age group from cradle roll to senior saints. Our children must get the message that church is a place to go to get your family split up.

Sunday school is a major culprit in this. I fully acknowledge that the intent of Sunday school is very good. I just question the method. When Dwight Moody was a young man in Chicago, he began his evangelism career bringing street kids to Sunday schools to be evangelized. Sunday school then operated on Sunday afternoons when the church families had already gone home from church. In this century, the Sunday school doesn't seem to know whether it is a greenhouse for Christian children or a mission station for the unsaved. The result is that the two are mixed and Christian parents take their children to Sunday school for teaching in godliness while the very setting makes them companions of children, some of whom are living in ungodly environments. At the same time, the system has separated the child of the Christian family from his parents so they aren't there to provide any guidance.

This whole business of bringing the people of the world into the meetings of the church disturbs me. The thrust of the church in the book of Acts was to go out and infiltrate the world. We seem to have the process reversed. We are bringing the world in to infiltrate the church. Particularly in the case of youth ministries, we are using some very worldly music and entertainments to attract attenders. The net result is the dilution of our message and the contamination of our spiritual state.

It seems that a major reorganization is in order. I suggest that we stop catering to the world's preference of separating the age groups. Let's devise some ministries to go out into the community and meet real needs with an emphasis on reaching heads of families. It's tempting to concentrate on children and youth, because they're usually more teachable and we find them less threatening. But I suspect much of the cause for the uncertainty some people feel concerning their salvation results from childhood conversion in families where there is no spiritual support. Of course, we should be eager to minister to any child with whom we come in contact. But I suspect things will fall into much better order if we concentrate our fire on adults, particularly men. If a man is genuinely converted, he will exert tremendous influence on his wife and children in a right direction.

I've mentioned the fact that we are diluting our message by making our church meetings comfortable for the uncommitted. Please don't react without thinking this through. Our purpose is not to make anybody uncomfortable, but the church family should be different from other social groups. A nonbeliever or unfaithful

Christian should be convicted by the godly example of dedicated believers, and shame on us if a man who is in rebellion to God can sit among us and be perfectly comfortable. No, I'm not saying we should exclude unbelievers from our meetings. My point is we need to drastically change our focus and concentrate on going out to meet needs wherever they are, rather than luring people into church services that are so watered down with compromising preaching and fleshly music that the spirit of the group brings no conviction.

The early church was different. Although the believers were being persecuted, their spiritual temperature was as it should have been. God was working supernaturally to meet needs and chasten sin. The community knew that these followers of the Way were different people. Even as God worked signs and wonders among them He punished the hypocrisy of Ananias and Sapphira with instant death. The result of this among the believers was that "...great fear came upon all the church.." (Acts 5:11) and "...of the rest durst no man join himself to them: but the people magnified them. And believers were the more added to the Lord, multitudes both of men and women (Acts 5:12,13)."

Let's understand the scenario. The church was busy going out into the community helping the sick and spiritually oppressed. God was strictly judging sin within the body, keeping it pure. Outsiders saw the power and holiness of God at work and no man dared to **join himself** to them, but **multitudes of believers were added to the Lord, of both men and women.** Worldly Christians were judged, outsiders were afraid to infiltrate, but the example of the pure church worked its intended purpose of conviction and conversion. Note too that it says both men and women were converted.

This is ideal, for as moms and dads go, so go their children-that is, if the parents are trained to lead their families aright.

Let's try to get back to a more Biblical pattern. We need to stop using the church to divide families, implying to children that their parents are not capable of training them spiritually without help. Let's train parents to train children so that our families can worship and learn together when the church meets. Let's design ministries to go out into the community and meet real needs rather than baiting unbelievers to come inside and hear our message in a watered-down spiritual atmosphere. Let's pray and work to reach adults, especially men, and then train them to lead their families in a Godly path. All this can be done without the complicated and inefficient apparatus encumbering the church at present. God's money will be better spent, believers will see that they, not the organization, are responsible to minister and parents will no longer have to protect their children from the influences of youth ministries designed to appeal to worldly kids and "bring them in."

Unless and until this change comes about, parents will have to withstand pressure to "support the church" by submitting their children to the many programs designed for them. We don't send our children to Sunday School, Awanas or youth activities (with the exception of those to which parents are invited). We feel that it is our responsibility to train our kids to serve God and if we fail, youth programs won't be able to make up the difference. In addition we believe we need to protect our children from addiction to peer status and the many other dangers of indiscriminate companionship.

Besides well-meaning people such as those in support groups and one's own church, there are plenty of other helpful souls who will assure you that it is socially destructive to "shelter" your children. Now let's stop and think this over a minute. Would it be so terrible if parents suddenly got less permissive and more protective? I don't know about you, but when I think about the big social problems of our time—AIDS, divorce, drug abuse, alcoholism, teen suicide, racial tension, oppressive government, occultism, humanism, abortion—I am hard pressed to think of any that seem to result from children spending too much time at home. As a matter of fact, I happen to believe that it is the breakdown of the family structure rather than the exaltation of it that is the great contributing factor here. I wonder how many people are now dying of AIDS or suffering from the physical and spiritual trauma of abortion, who wish their parents hadn't been so protective?

One line of reasoning we hear from the un-protectors says that kids have to make their own mistakes. They can't live by their parents' values and guidance forever. They have to experiment. They have to learn it all by experience.

Uh, excuse me. Did you learn that it's unwise to stand in front of a speeding truck—by experience?

If there is one thing the youth of this country clearly need, it is more, not less guidance from their parents. Some are making an effort toward this through education and so forth, but we know we can't trust the educational system. God has put children in families under parents in large part so that they would be protected. "But they need to experience the real world, to learn how to deal with what's out there." True. They need to learn to drive, too. But there's a right time, place and method. Besides, sometimes the appropriate way to "deal with" something is avoidance. We wouldn't want our children to learn to deal with sharks by swimming with them or with poison by swallowing it.

It's not always easy to do what you believe is best for your children. The tide of opinion can be pretty hard to swim against. Some people are threatened by your example, wondering if they should consider making some similar changes for their own children. Most public and private school people will think you're depriving your children socially. Your church leaders and friends may feel a certain amount of rejection when you decline to place your kids in "their" programs.

Some of the hardest resistance to handle often comes from those nearest and dearest. When Marilyn and I decided on home education for our children, both our families were supportive. The idea struck them as a little revolutionary (especially back then) but they all knew Marilyn was excellent with children and had done well in school herself, having considerable experience student teaching and a year of college toward a teaching degree before she threw her life away and married me. But our experience, unfortunately, has not been typical of all parents who selected home education.

We have heard from a number of couples that Armageddon erupted when their parents heard of their plans to home educate. Grandparents do, after all, cherish exalted notions of achievement and prominence for their grandchildren. And it can be pretty hard to either avoid your parents entirely or ignore all their little hints to the effect that "Johnny's really becoming a Mommy's boy," etc. The ideal scenario is for grandparents to live locally, be wildly enthusiastic about home education and eagerly offer to help with instruction and keep the kids for your weekly date night with your spouse. But ideals are rarely realized and many parents endure some antagonism from Grandma and Grandpa.

It's important that you treat your parents with respect. Your treatment of them is teaching your children volumes about how they are one day to treat you. If they are unfavorable to your plans, do your best to make peace. If they have honest reservations about the feasibility of teaching at home, find some documentation that shows the success of home education nationwide. If they worry about the social aspects—well, give them this book if it's not too extreme for them. Explain what you have seen in school that you believe impacts children negatively. Be loving and patient with them. If it seems appropriate, ask them to delay forming an opinion for a year or two until they've had a chance to see for themselves what the real results of home education are. There is a Biblical principle here, as illustrated in Daniel 1:12,13.

Family and close friends can present some of the worst pressure to conform, as we can testify. As I said before, our families support our home teaching but the fact that we don't have a television, don't use birth control and don't take our children to Sunday school is a bit hard for many relatives and friends to swallow.

A friend told me recently that she appreciated the fact that we had "gone before" her and her husband in establishing a conservative lifestyle for our children. She said that were it not for our example, she didn't think they would have had the courage to stand against the pressure to expose their children to the usual social experiences. Well, it's nice to be appreciated. Just the fact that we have twelve children has let us in for a fair amount of criticism and we have also had the less-than-pleasant distinction of defending our convictions in court.

In a way, our whole generation seems called to blaze a trail. Nearly all of us attended public school, listened to rock music and played the big social game. Now we are the parents, and having lived as young people through the sick sixties and seventies, are feeling a need to revert to a more conservative lifestyle. We are opting for private school or home education, turning off the TV, breast feeding and questioning some social traditions such as dating. Today's home educators are establishing, by trial and error, a foundation on which we hope our children will build self-perpetuating godly generations. It is well that we are doing so, because our society is sick and dying, following the pattern of earlier nations that have turned away from God and rotted away. The social engineers are willing to try anything but the Biblical plan of building families and the educators can't think of anything better than giving away condoms in the schools. Change toward sanity must come quickly and our best, and perhaps only, hope is for Christian home educators to raise up a nationwide standard of godliness and let other elements of society aspire or react to it as they will. It isn't easy to live in the lunatic fringe, but it's easier now than it was ten years ago and it will be still less difficult in the future. As there are more and more of us, the fringe gets wider and as it does, others consider us less lunatic.

Personally, I find it ironic that we are considered strange by some, when all we want is what they themselves often wish for—a simpler, calmer, more family-oriented mode of living. I often find myself sighing for the days when the Boyers had less social contact than we do now.

Recently, Marilyn and I took a nostalgic drive through our old neighborhood. Concord is a tiny village about ten miles from the city limits in a very rural area. It was just past Concord, in a small development of FmHA homes, that we bought our first house.   It was in the third year of our marriage. We had only two children, Rickey at a year and a half and baby Timmy, age two months. When we moved our shabby furniture into that tiny but brand new yellow house, we were fresh escapees from trailer park living and really feeling our oats. As the months went by, the driveway gravel settled a bit, we grew our first garden and our little yellow house became home, complete with little finger smudges on the cheap paint of the walls and doorways. It was wonderful to have a real house, one that didn't tremble when the dog trotted through the living room and on whose wall one could hang a picture without the point of the nail showing outside the house.

During the four years we lived there at Concord I went through some trauma in my underdeveloped career, trying this and that to "find myself" in a line of work that suited. But our home life had a quality of steadiness that has been hard to duplicate since. Marilyn's responsibilities were basically limited to taking care of me, our little boys and the little yellow house. Our social life revolved around our church fellowship and a few neighborhood friends. The phone didn't ring off the hook as it does now and visitors were not common. My wife had time to minister to our two, then three, then four little boys individually each day and it was during those years that she began creating the spiritual training projects that never fail to excite and inspire the moms at our seminars. Life was peaceful except for my job-related frustrations and home was a haven for the nerves.

These days we're busy people, raising teenagers as well as little ones, running a business, doing seminars, writing books and magazine articles. Life is interesting and challenging and I like it, although I could stand a bit more sleep sometimes.

The Socialization Trap

We're not the only home educators around any more and it isn't always a pleasure to watch dedicated young parents, trying only to give their children the best learning possible, burden themselves and their families with a schedule that makes one weary to hear about it. If only we could reach them all, to tell them what we've learned the hard way—that there's no place like home.

Times have changed for our family. A lot of water has gone over the dam since we left that first home of our own. But in my mind there is etched forever a picture of a little yellow house on a corner lot. A pretty young lady is hanging clothes on a line in the shade of two huge old cherry trees. Four little boys are playing in a sandbox and on the grass. There is a garden by the road and a big, red dog sleeping in the sun. It's a scene that looks more like home with each year that goes by.

Chapter 2

A Good Example of a Bad Example

It may be that the most remarkable thing about the Christian home education movement today is that we have chosen such a remarkably bad example for our socialization model. The fact that we are socializing our children in essentially the same process as the rest of our society suggests that we see nothing seriously wrong with the human aspects of that society. I think this demonstrates a significant degree of spiritual and intellectual myopia on our part.

American society is morally and spiritually bankrupt. Since the ludicrous Roe vs. Wade decision in January of 1973 we have legally murdered twenty-five million human beings in this country. That is *ten percent of our present population*. This slaughter is predicated on the distinction between a "human being" and something called a in legal terms a "person." The capacity for rational thought is obviously on the wane in our country.

But abortion, outrageous as it is, represents only a tip of the iceberg. There now exist in this country a multiplicity of social problems that spell national disaster if the trend is not reversed. It is critically important that home educators learn to look to the principles of Scripture, rather than to the community around them, for a pattern of social success and health.

Former Secretary of Education William Bennett has done us another invaluable service with his recent publication of a report entitled the *Index of Leading Cultural Indicators*. This report, produced by the Heritage Foundation, a tax-exempt public policy research institute, demonstrates vividly the social rot eating at America's soul. I'm taking the liberty of quoting at some length from it, as its data are very current and it deals with social issues that are much in the forefront of public debate.

In his introduction Dr. Bennett says:

> Over the last three decades we have experienced substantial social regression. Today the forces of social decomposition are challenging—and in some instances, overtaking—the forces of social composition. And when decomposition takes hold, it exacts an enormous human cost.
>
> Since 1960, population has increased 41 percent; the Gross Domestic Product has nearly tripled; and total social spending by all levels of government (measured in constant 1990 dollars) has risen from $143.73 billion to $787.0 billion-

more than a five-fold increase. Inflation-adjusted spending on welfare has increased 630 percent and inflation-adjusted spending on education has increased 225 percent. The United States has the strongest economy in the world, a healthy entrepreneurial spirit, a still-healthy work ethic, and a generous attitude—good signs all.

But during the same 30-year period there has been a 560 percent increase in violent crime; more than a 400 percent increase in illegitimate births; a quadrupling in divorce rates; a tripling of the percentage of children living in single-parent homes; more than a 200 percent increase in the teenage suicide rate; and a drop of almost 80 points in the SAT scores. Modern-day social pathologies, at least great parts of them, have gotten worse. They seem impervious to government spending on their alleviation, even very large amounts of spending.[1]

A teacher survey done in the public schools in 1940 listed as the top school problems: talking out of turn, chewing gum, making noise, running in halls, cutting in line, dress code infractions, littering. Fifty years later, the teachers of 1990 listed drug abuse, alcohol abuse, pregnancy, suicide, rape, robbery and assault.

With the constant deluge of bad news pouring out of radio and television speakers and plastered across the pages of newspapers it is easy to become desensitized to the real condition of American society. In the following paragraphs I will use Bennett's report to paint a picture of the true state of things as far as statistics can do so. Try to read this with your mind open and sensitive to what the numbers mean in terms of human lives affected.

Crime: Since 1960, the nation's population has increased only 41 percent. Total crimes have increased by 300 percent and violent crime has grown by 500 percent. Our rate of violent crime is now worse than in any other industrialized country in the world.

Some social "experts" blame the rise in crime on poverty. It is in the poor neighborhoods, they say, that crime is at its worst. This is silly. The fact that crime and poverty coexist does not prove a cause and effect relationship. However, Scripture indicates that such a relationship does exist, with the notable difference that it is not a situation of poverty causing crime, but that the reverse is true. Proverbs 13:25 says, "The righteous man has enough to satisfy his appetite, but the stomach of the wicked is in want." Were we not such ahistorical thinkers we would have only to look back to the 1930's and the Great Depression for proof of this. During the Depression, the United States experienced 25 percent unemployment—a much higher rate than today—and many other symptoms of hard times that are unknown to us, yet the crime rate was much lower. Our crime problem today is not that we have more problems, but that we have trained ourselves to blame our problems on others and use them for an excuse to do what we want to do.

A particularly disturbing aspect of the rise in the crime rate is that the greatest percentage increase in crimes of violence is taking place among the young. Using statistics provided by the FBI, Bennett notes that juvenile crime nearly quadrupled between 1965 and 1990. This increase, the FBI said, was not restricted to inner city minority youth but represented a cross section of all races, social classes and lifestyles.

Another symptom of the national sickness is the rate of **teen pregnancy, birth and abortion.** Quoting a study entitled "Teen Sex" in *The American Enterprise,* Jan/Feb 1993, Bennett says:

> The number of unmarried teenagers getting pregnant has nearly doubled in the past two decades...Rare in the early 1960's, by the late 1980's nearly one unmarried teenage girl in ten got pregnant.
>
> Births to all unmarried women of childbearing age in 1990 represented a 28% illegitimacy rate, with the rate soaring to an unbelievable 65.2 % among black women.

Teen suicide is much in the news these days. The teen suicide rate has more than tripled since 1960. Suicide is second only to accidents (particularly motor vehicle accidents) as a cause of death among adolescents. And who knows how many auto "accidents" that kill teens were in fact acts of suicide?

Divorce is now down slightly in America., but so is the number of marriages per year. In 1991 there were 2,433,00 marriages and 1,168,000 divorces. Nearly half as many people got divorced in 1991 as got married and that does not reflect the couples living together outside of wedlock. Fewer than 60 percent of American children today are living with their biological, married parents.

Is education the answer to social problems? Apparently not. Bennett's report shows that more people than ever before are graduating from high school, although with the social promotions, abysmal functional illiteracy among graduates and the fact that almost 9 of 10 high school seniors have used alcohol, one's confidence in a high school diploma may be less than it once was.

In short, Bennett's report of America's cultural indicators shows that our society has become a moral quagmire. Most of us are still shocked although we hear sad statistics often, and numbers cannot reflect the misery of a drug addict or tears on the face of a child. But if there is one conclusion that can safely be drawn from this report it is that there is something dreadfully wrong with the way modern Americans are learning to act as members of society. It is critical that Christian home educators wake up and realize that the socialization of our children must be pursued in a purposeful manner and based on the standards of Scripture, not contemporary society.

GOD'S WAY VS. MAN'S WAY

I believe that the social failure of our society reflects the failure of the church to provide salt and light to the world around us. Light is for illuminating truth and revealing the path. Salt is a cleansing and preserving agent. It kills bacteria and protects against putrefaction. The rottenness of our social structure is due to the lack of savor in the salt of the nation. That is the reason for both the social rot and the growing persecution of Christians. We have lost our savor and are being trodden under foot.

Thankfully, many believers, particularly those in the home education movement, are beginning to raise up a godly standard once again by rebuilding God's chosen social unit, the family. We are beginning to turn back to absolute moral standards, closer family relationships and parental responsibility for child training.

The next major step, as I see it, is for home educators to begin building healthy social environments for our children to grow up in. This is still one of the major blind spots of the movement. We have taken our children out of an unhealthy social atmosphere by keeping them out of school. Now we must replace that setting with a social life that will encourage rather than detract from a godly worldview.

As I said before, one of the myths surrounding home education says that children who are not in school are socially deprived and it is therefore important for parents to provide for their children to have plenty of time with kids their own age . We make this false assumption only because it reflects what we have seen done to children all our lives in schools. It's hard for us to imagine any other social structure for childhood.

But there is such a structure and it not only includes mixing the age groups but a number of other healthy features as well. A plan for healthy social development is given in the Scriptures if we will but recognize the principles when we see them. Let's take a look at God's way of socializing children and compare it with man's way.

> Man's way: Segregate age groups from each
>   other.
> God's way: Mix the age groups.
>
> Man's way: Seek companions for my pleasure
>   and advantage.
> God's way: Seek companions to edify and be
>   edified.

Man's way: Set no character standards for
            potential companions.
God's way: Be wary of potential companions
            without godly standards.

Man's way: Develop independent spirit
            toward family
God's way: Grow in family unity.

Man's way: Lack of respect for parents.
God's way: Respect authority of parents.

Man's way: Selfishly motivated social
            contact.
God's way: Service-oriented social contact.

Man's way: Learn contempt for those older
            and younger than one's self.
God's way: Learn respect for the aged and
            tenderness for the young.

Man's way: Random social exposure.
God's way: Guided social exposure.

This last point rather sums up the Boyers' philosophy of social contact. The idea of letting our children spend extended time with any person with whom they might come in contact is as foreign to us as the idea of flying to the moon in a washing machine. The fact is that people, and especially young people, tend to grow attached to those with whom they spend their time. This attachment is as healthy or unhealthy as the spiritual influence exerted by the other person in the relationship. In her book, *Life in the*

30

Classroom and Playground, Bronwyn Davies talks about this tendency to develop a liking for those with whom we share time:

> Adults assume that the reason friendships develop is that people like one another. They construe their own friendships as developing from reciprocated feelings of attraction. Children, in contrast, while they do not negate liking as having some considerable importance, see proximity, or being with someone, as the first and basic element of friendships. Homans, in contrast with many social psychologists, would tend to agree with the children, that the nature of the other is no more (and perhaps less) important than the fact of being with the other. He says, 'an increase of interaction between persons is accompanied by an increase of sentiments of friendliness between them.' In other words, we come to like the people we associate with because we associate with them, rather than because they are intrinsically likeable. He goes on to say, 'You can get to like some pretty queer customers if you go around with them long enough. Their queerness becomes irrelevant.' [2]

Exactly. And this is why responsible Christian parents don't let their child's social world develop at random. Our society is so pervasively corrupt—even though we have grown so desensitized we sometimes forget it—that we cannot trust our children to relationships built on chance association. Today, as never before in America, the stakes are just too high.

Chapter 3

What Happens in Peer Groups

You've heard it time and time again. You mention that you've decided to teach your children at home and somebody goes apoplectic. "How will your children learn to get along with other people?" "How will they know how to deal with real life?" "How will they get enough contact with kids their own age?"

The assumption of course is that there is something about a social group made up of children all the same age that is magic for a child's soul. The facts are to the contrary. An age peer group is about the worst age arrangement for healthy social development. The thing that has had Marilyn and me tearing our hair out for years is that home educators are not much easier to convince of this than are school educators and skeptical grandparents. Moms and dads continue to remove their children from school, often mainly because of what this cherubic crowd is doing to their children socially, then turn right around and involve them in a multitude of activities centered around an age peer situation.

What I hope to do in this chapter is demonstrate that an age peer social group is harmful and that it is the last thing a parent really wants to create for his child. I'll do this by listing some of the problems of age-peer socialization and then offering some amplification and documentation of each problem. I hope this will provide you with assurance that what you are doing as a home educator-if you are also protecting your child from peer groups outside the classroom-is right, and with some ammunition for use in discussions with critics who have minds open enough to give you an honest hearing.

1. Peer group socialization tends to make children dependent on their peers.

A book I found in a college library appears to be a college-level sociology text. Published in 1986, it is fairly up to date and very revealing in stating the humanist view on the function of peer groups:

> The peer group helps children form attitudes and values. It provides a filter for sifting through their parent-derived values *and deciding which ones to keep and which to discard* (italics mine).[1]

Did that register with you? These authors are saying that not only is it a fact, but it is desirable that children look to their peers for approval or rejection of the values their parents are teaching in the home!

The authors go on to say quite correctly,

> Peer groups often impose their values on the emerging individual. Children play games in groups...Unfortunately it's usually in the company of friends that children also shoplift, begin to smoke and drink, sneak into the movies, and do other undesirable things. Sixth graders who are rated as more 'peer-oriented' report engaging in more of this kind of behavior than 'parent-oriented' children (Condry, et al., 1968).[2]

Further, the authors state, again rightly,

> We all want people to like us. What our peers think of us matters terribly. Our acceptance by others affects our present happiness, and it may well echo through the years to affect our well-being.[3]

All the more reason we should not let our children mingle indiscriminately with others, getting random mixtures of responses to their worth as perceived by any one who cares to make a compliment or insult.

2. Peer socialization subjects children to constant attacks on their self-esteem.

These same authors say something that should give every parent food for thought:

> The peer group provides children with a more realistic gauge for the development of skills and abilities than the parents, who are so much bigger and wiser and more powerful, or than baby brothers and sisters. Only within a large group of peers can children get a sense of how smart, how athletic, how skillful and how personable they are.[4]

In other words, peer groups give our children opportunity to develop opinions of themselves based on how they compare to others. How this constant comparison and competition is supposed to help is a mystery. It's certainly a contrast to the assurances of Scripture (cf Psalm 139) that each of us is a unique individual, created carefully and specially by a loving God. "For we are not bold to class or compare ourselves with some of those who commend themselves; but when they measure themselves by themselves, and compare themselves with themselves, they are without understanding. But HE WHO BOASTS, LET HIM BOAST IN THE LORD. For not he who commends himself is approved, but whom the Lord commends (IICor. 10:12,17,18)."

Education reformer John Holt writes:

> When I point out to people that the social life of most schools and classrooms is mean-spirited, status-oriented, competitive, and snobbish, I am always astonished by their response. Not one person of the hundreds with whom I've discussed

this has yet said to me that the social life at school is kindly, generous, supporting, democratic, friendly, loving, or good for children. No, without exception, when I condemn the social life of school, people say, "But that's what the children are going to meet in Real Life."[5]

Those people are wrong. The social pressure in school peer groups is much greater than that which most adults face. Only among children is it acceptable to insult and ridicule each other loudly and frequently. Among adults, it would quickly lead to altercations, possibly violence and certainly the breaking of relationships. Of course, adults differ from children in that adults have a choice of people with whom to associate. School children are locked in.

A reader of Holt's *Growing Without Schooling* wrote, "This morning I asked my third graders, 'Do you feel that in our school kids are nice, kind to each other?' Out of 22 kids, only two felt that they saw kindness, and the rest felt most kids are mean, call names, hurt feelings, etc. Frankly I was amazed. I have always felt our school is a uniquely friendly place..."[6]

John Taylor Gatto, 1991 New York State Teacher of the Year, has this to say about the relationship of children to each other based on 26 years of teaching:

> The children I teach are cruel to each other; they lack compassion for misfortune; they laugh at weakness, they have contempt for people whose need for help shows too plainly.[7]

At a Learning Parent seminar in North Carolina a man came up to me during a break and related to me the story of a fourteen-year-old boy he knew who had begged his mother to teach him at home because of the social pressure at school. This boy was unaccepted by the crowd for some reason and felt the rejection deeply. He persisted in his pleas to his mother but she had a career that meant a lot to her and evidently didn't feel the problem was as serious as her son described it. The episode continued for some time and ended tragically when the boy committed suicide. Most children don't react so desperately to peer pressure, but the story of this young man illustrates the devastating pressure of peer contact in concentrated doses.

3. Peer socialization creates negative attitudes toward other age groups.

When I was an adolescent in school it was generally understood that our age group was at the pinnacle of human quality. Younger children, particularly our own siblings, were nuisances, parasites whose interests were silly and whose abilities were so inferior to ours that there was just no hope they would ever catch up. Adults were hopelessly out of touch with reality; parents in their Stone Age stupor couldn't be expected to understand what life was all about and teachers sought and took jobs in schools just for the pleasure of torturing children. Older kids were sometimes ok, even admirable, but often arrogant and threatening. This was particularly true of older brothers when in the company of their friends.

I remember walking down the hall in our high school with my friend Jeff, also a freshman. As we passed a group of older boys coming the other way, a fist shot out of the group and gave Jeff a hard punch on the shoulder. The fist belonged to Jeff's older brother. Evidently he had taken the opportunity to enhance his standing with his buddies by demonstrating his sense of humor. Jeff didn't seem to see the joke. I can still recall the hurt in his eyes.

It is significant that this contempt for younger children is not natural, as evidenced by other societies. In the former Soviet Union for example, school classes of children would "adopt" classes of younger children for the purpose of providing them with reinforcement of state-mandated behavior. This and other efforts to mingle the age groups resulted in social phenomena that would surprise most American observers. Psychologist Urie Bronfenbrenner reported an event that took place during a visit to Russia:

> I recall an incident which occurred on a Moscow street. Our youngest son—then four—was walking briskly a pace or two ahead of us when from the opposite direction there came a company of teenage boys. The first one no sooner spied Stevie than he opened his arms wide and, calling "Ai, malysh!" (Hey, little one!), scooped him up, hugged him, kissed him resoundingly, and passed him on to the rest of the company, who did likewise, and then began a merry children's dance, as they caressed him with words and gestures. Similar behavior on the part of an American adolescent male would surely prompt his parents to consult a psychiatrist.[8]

It is normal, natural and Scriptural for human beings to exhibit tenderness toward the young and respect for the old. These traits are an integral part of most cultures who do not separate their young by age groups for education. We have our practice of age segregation to thank for our problem of age alienation.

> Schools socially stratify the youth beginning the first year, and the social stratification intensifies each year. By the time the children are in junior high, they have no idea how to socialize with anyone outside of their peer group. The very idea of socializing with anyone not their own age is appalling to these children. They are unable to enter into the simplest conversation with any adults or younger children. When they finally graduate from high school, and enter the society at large, they have to spend several years re-adjusting their attitudes until they can fit in. Some never do.[9]

4. Peer socialization breaks down family relationships.

Harmful as it is for children to grow up alienated from other age groups, this syndrome finds its worst effect in the emotional separation of children from other members of their own family. Peer dependency separates kids both from their siblings and their parents through time commitments, interests and emotional bonding.

A study was done on this subject by Dr. Urie Bronfenbrenner of Cornell University and his colleagues. Bronfenbrenner writes about the results:

> In general, the peer-oriented children held rather negative views of themselves and the peer group. They also expressed a dim view of their

own future. Their parents were rated as lower than those of the adult-oriented children both in the expression of affection and support, and in the exercise of discipline and control. Finally, in contrast to the adult-oriented group, the peer-oriented children report engaging in more antisocial behavior such as "doing something illegal," "playing hooky," lying, teasing other children, etc.[10]

Bronfenbrenner goes on to say the study indicated that the peer dependency of the children surveyed resulted in large part from parental disregard, evidence that the replacement of parent dependency with peer dependency is a two-way street causatively. That is, while peer dependency robs parents of some of their child's affection, it is also true that a lack of parental affection and involvement can cause a child to grow peer dependent.

Although much attention is given to the problem of peer pressure, Americans today seem to worry lest their children become too parent dependent. This would have been foreign to the Jews of Bible times. Old Testament Scriptures caution young men to pay attention to the counsel of their parents even when they themselves are adults and their parents are old. Proverbs 23:22 is characteristic: "Listen to your father who begot you, And do not despise your mother when she is old."

In that culture, it was standard practice for parents to care for their children while they were young and children to care for parents when old age arrived. Grandparents were revered and uncles, aunts and cousins contributed to the makeup of the child's social circle. The situation was not so very different in our own country a generation ago. Unfortunately for all of us, this has changed radically.

Today some parents actually place their children in child care in order to make them less parent dependent. Marilyn and I once had dinner with another couple who don't share much of our frame of reference on the subject of child rearing. During the course of the evening the conversation turned to babies and our lady friend mentioned that she was looking for a sitter to keep her 14-month-old daughter because "she's getting too attached to Mama." It sounded to me like a blatant excuse for Mama to get more independent of Baby, but the fact that Mama could even suggest excessive parent dependency as a reason to seek child care hints at the sickness in the institution of family life in our day. Wouldn't it be awful if babies grew dependent on their mothers?

It is also troubling that siblings don't like the company of each other more than they do. I recall hearing a man tell how, when he was a young teenager his parents made his older brother drive him to school. The older boy, a student at the same high school, made his younger sibling hide in the back seat when they approached the school so none of his friends would see him driving around with his little brother.

Sadder yet was a story told to us by a couple who came to us for help in starting to home educate. The father had been the administrator and teacher in a tiny church school in Pennsylvania before moving to our city. He and his wife told us that their children had always been close to their parents and each other until they moved here and enrolled their children in a large Christian school. One evening after church the mother picked up their two-year-old from the nursery and was carrying him toward the exit when they passed her fifteen-year-old son standing with a group of his new school friends in the hall. As they passed, the little boy saw his brother, leaned out to reach for him and called out to him. The older boy quickly turned away and pretended he hadn't heard, a crushing blow to his baby brother. A narrow escape from having his macho friends find out that he actually cared about his little brother.

One man said, "Whenever any of my older brother's friends were at our house or my name was mentioned among them, my brother felt obligated to say something about how stupid I was. I was twelve years old before I found out my name wasn't Stupid."

5. Peer socialization isolates children from the real "adult" world.

John Taylor Gatto says,

> ...the children I teach are indifferent to the adult world. This defies the experience of thousands of years. A close study of what big people were up to was always the most exciting occupation of youth, but nobody wants children to grow up these days, least of all the children..."[11]

There is an interesting and disturbing contradiction here. On the one hand, as Gatto says, we try to prevent children from growing up. We keep them in school as long as possible, as if we felt that the longer we kept them out of adult society, the better they would be prepared for it. At the same time, we are robbing them of their youthful innocence by introducing them to sex education, death education, etc., at ever younger ages. It's as if we want to split our children in half, with one part growing old before its time and the other forever frozen in a world of skateboards and Ninja turtles.

This is important. In fact I think this is a great problem to which we must find a solution if we are to save our society. Eighteen-year-olds now have the vote, but most of them don't know how or for whom to vote. Most of them don't seem to care much, and this reflects a much broader don't-care attitude to the really important things pertaining to life in this society.

Adults today don't seem to expect high school graduates to be adults, ready to accept adult responsibility and with adult interests and concerns. John Quincy Adams, whose father was a diplomat before becoming president, spent his youth among brilliant and important adults rather than segregated within his own age group. He traveled to a number of foreign countries with the elder Adams and at age fourteen was secretary to the American minister to Russia. Nowadays fourteen-year-olds generally are considered young children and even those mature enough to kill somebody are usually not tried as adults for that very adult crime. I heard recently that about ninety percent of college seniors don't know what they want to do after graduation. Surely there's a connection between their years-long sequestration from society in school peer groups and their lack of interest and capability in adult affairs.

We could learn a lot about the difference between adults and almost-adults if we could crawl inside the heads of people and compare their thought patterns. I suspect that would give us a bold illustration of the difference between the attitudes of the generations. What do adults think about? Among other things, they think about their work, finances, health, their family responsibilities, maintaining their homes. They think about politics and social conditions. They think about the needs of others and the ministries of their churches. They think about things of lasting importance.

What do almost-adults think about? For instance, seventeen-year-old high school seniors. They think about their nice cars, or the nice cars they'd like to have. They think about who is dating whom. They wonder about the grade they will get on the exam—though few ever wonder what they are learning that will be of any use twenty years (or for that matter twenty hours) after the exam is over.

They are careful to appear in uniform: proper name brands and correct mode of wear (currently in our area it's in vogue to wear a jacket, sweatshirt or sweater with one shoulder exposed. If they only knew how stupid it makes them look.) They think about attending the game Friday night and some of them think about their role in it, basing their self-esteem on whether they get to play and how well they do. Sometimes they think about what college to go to, although few will complete four years in the school they expect to attend and fewer still will pursue the same major through the entire time. They think about having or not having homework done, about the next party or dance and about who will have a date for the prom. Very often, if you could read their minds you would find them thinking about what others think of them.

Yet it is also true that in some respects we try to hurry our children. We start them in school before most of them can handle the separation from Mom, the boring routine, enforced inactivity and pressure of constant comparison (not that these things are ever very good for anybody). Some parents prime their little girls for a life of worldly narcissism by grooming them for "Little Miss" pageants. Some times dads push boys into Little League and other competitive sports, perhaps hoping for vicarious fulfillment of the dreams of glory that never came true in their own amateur athletic careers. Tiny tots are taken to sitters and day care centers years before they can manage the stress of several hours at a time away from home.

We have created a trend of perverting childhood and we can only reverse it by returning to a Scriptural and natural understanding of childhood's purpose. The purpose of childhood is to prepare people for adulthood. By this we should know better than to separate children from adult companionship. It is hard to prepare anyone to fit into something to which they have little exposure.

I recently read an excellent article on the women's movement and the men's movement that seems to be beginning as a response to it. They're now doing weekend retreats for groups of men who want to relish being men. Evidently considerable numbers of middle-aged executives are spending weekends sleeping in tents, cooking over campfires and beating tomtoms. The theme seems to be that there is much healthy male bonding to be had in teepees full of paunchy, shirtless, balding office types beating drums and presumably, occasionally their chests. I don't know enough about this movement to comment much on it, but the author of the article seemed unimpressed. He described the leader of the movement, whose name I can't recall, as a septuagenarian Wally Cox.

I mention this article because of the excellent analogy its conclusion offers to age segregation. The author concludes by saying that the men's movement, like the women's movement to which it seems to be a reaction, is off target. He points out that the genders do not find their fulfillment in separation unto themselves, but in joining together with the opposite gender. It is, he says, not in segregation but in blending together that the two sexes find their true identity and fulfillment. His argument makes all kinds of sense.

The same logic applies to integration of the age groups. Children are born into the healthiest social situation in existence and we spend the rest of their growing up years moving them out of it. It's in the home and in the company of others of various ages that people realize the fullness of their natural proclivity toward older and younger people. Children learn better at home than anywhere else that older people are to be respected and younger people are to b e cared for.

Of course, nobody lives exclusively at home and so a balanced life includes involvement in the affairs of the church, neighborhood, workplace and marketplace. But the home is the greenhouse in which baby humans are nurtured until they are strong enough to withstand the elements outside.

I once planted some tomato plants a little too early, hoping to give them a headstart. But the early spring weather wasn't yet warm enough, so the plants were shocked by their premature exposure. They survived, but another batch of plants I planted two weeks later caught up and passed the first ones in development. The first bunch grew more slowly, were less luxuriant and bore less fruit. They never did reach their full potential. I had tried to give them a head start but in doing so I harmed them irreversibly.

We have now done the same thing to at least two generations of American children. We have removed them from the greenhouse too early and into the wrong conditions for growth. We shouldn't be surprised that, when their bodies are fully mature, their souls are puny and stunted, incapable of bearing adult fruit.

PART II: SCHOOL AND SOCIALIZATION

Chapter 4

Adults in School

Most of us can recall one or more adults from our school days who were good for us. We should all be thankful that education attracts many people who are there because they love children and want to help them. I'll always have fond memories of the English teacher I had in my senior year of high school. Her name was Adonna Blair and she was my favorite teacher. I think I was one of her favorites too, because she put up with me. I was a bit of a class clown (somebody has to do it) and I spent most of the class period sitting on the waste basket by her desk keeping her company. Sometimes I'd actually do some work with my books on the end of her desk; other times I would volunteer my help in directing class discussions. When I had a character role in the school play she told me the next day in front of the whole class that I had been by far the best performer on stage. She encouraged me to go on to college even though I hated school and if I remember correctly even wrote me a recommendation, which must have stretched her imagination severely. Miss Blair wrote to me the summer after I graduated and I wrote back, but we eventually lost touch. But though she left the old high school long before a class reunion brought me back, I remember her well and her confidence in me despite my obnoxious behavior is still an encouragement today. If you ever read this, Miss Blair, I wish you'd drop me a line. I'd like to say thank you.

One of the significant school adults other than my own teachers was a special education teacher named Jackson. Mr. Jackson somehow got elected to drive me home one day in sixth grade when I was sick with the flu or something. I had to ask him to stop just after we got off the school grounds so I could throw up. It wasn't much fun. But he got out of the car with me and as I stood bent over in the ditch heaving miserably, he put his hand on my back and with the other, supported my forehead. I don't remember a word Mr. Jackson ever said to me but the touch of a compassionate adult is something that sticks in a child's mind. Sometimes for thirty years.

I knew other kind, encouraging adults in school. Mr. Muir appreciated the stories I wrote. Mr. Smith, the assistant principal, treated me with respect. Coach Stranathan laughed at my pranks.

I know other sincere teachers now, too. Our church has a Christian school and I know some of their staff and teachers. I'm very impressed with their dedication and the relationship they have with the students. Through various business and other contacts I've met a number of other educators, too, and I've shed the prejudice that all public school teachers are humanist subversives.

But all the adults who impacted me positively in school have not taken away the memory of the ones who affected me otherwise. Some of my memories are no doubt very inaccurate these many years later, but accurate or not they have stayed with me.

As early as the second grade I made the acquaintance of the school gestapo. My teacher, Mrs. Franklin, was one of those who used ridicule and cutting remarks to keep order. I've seen her ignore a child who was trying to speak to her even though she was clearly available to answer him, just because she didn't like the way he addressed her. I used to make good use of quiet class time by practicing holding my breath and timing myself by the classroom clock. I got rather good at it, but when Mrs. Franklin discovered me a quiet reproof wasn't sufficient. She had to call me to the attention of the entire class. Mrs. Franklin had pets, snooty little girls who finished their assignments early and got to do special projects to help Teacher. They weren't corrected when a couple of them would meet at the wastebasket on the pretense of discarding trash paper and gossip. The same bunch were the ones who gathered around her desk on the last day of school, drooling servilely and telling her what a good teacher she was. I had nothing but contempt for these sycophants and the only farewell wish I had for Teacher was that I would never see her again.

As I prepared to enter third grade, I hated the thought of going back to school but at least I had the assurance that my teacher couldn't be as bad as the one of the previous year. I was right. She was worse.

Miss Tinker was an old maid who wore thick-soled shoes, her watch on the inside of her wrist and a sweater with sleeves pulled up revealing muscular forearms. She didn't talk to me much that I can recall, but she managed to constantly communicate to me that she just couldn't quite believe how stupid I was. When my mother went into her classroom on parent-teacher conference night Miss Tinker turned to her from the window where she had been gazing outside and without preamble or greeting said, "Your son is downright poky!" Such a charmer.

The first day of fourth grade rolled around (despite fervent prayer) and as I bade farewell to my summer freedom I had at least the consolation of knowing that whoever my new teacher was, she had to be an improvement over the previous two. Such is the incurable optimism of youth. Guess who got transferred that year from teaching second grade to teaching fourth?

The only scene I remember from Mrs. Franklin's performance in fourth grade is the time Glenn got in trouble. Glenn was a meek and very insecure boy who was so self-conscious that he couldn't stand the molecule of attention drawn to himself by getting up to go to the waste basket. Instead he would wad up discarded sheets of paper and shove them down inside his pants. The memory of Mrs. Franklin's response when she noticed this brings tears to my eyes even as I write about it. She called the attention of the entire class to it and proceeded to heap ridicule on Glenn. The little sinner slid down in his seat and tried desperately to look in any other direction than at anybody. His mortification was palpable as he squirmed, shuffled his feet and agitatedly gnawed his lower lip. Several years ago I related this incident to a friend of mine, a teacher and school administrator for sixteen years. He said, "Rick, that happens hundreds of times a day in classrooms all across America." No doubt it does. Which is one more reason I will never send my children to school.

Could the frustration resulting from this type of emotional abuse be part of the reason for delinquency? I suspect so. John Holt once wrote that he felt that the reason school buildings were so often the target of vandalism was that children so resent what is done to them in school. They see the entire plant—building, grounds, equipment—as an instrument of mistreatment and confinement. Of course this is not true of all children; some like going to school. But for those who don't, the adults who hurt them are above retaliation. The physical edifice that surrounds the process is used as a scapegoat for the resentment of the vandals.

James Marshall comments on this in his book, *The Devil in the Classroom:*

> One cannot help but be teased by evidence that young people with a high delinquency rate tend to be less delinquent after they have left school than before. The Vera Institute of Justice (Strasburg 1978) has found that delinquents who left school had higher "police contact rates" while they were in school than did students who remained in school. However, after they had left school their contact rates declined sharply. The students who continued in school, however, had increases in their police contacts.[1]

I know a little girl in the third grade who was refused permission to go to the bathroom and as a result had an accident in class. I've been a long time out of elementary school but I think I can partially imagine her embarrassment. The attention of the other children, having one's mother called from work to bring a change of clothes. It would take a while to live that one down. The girl's mother had a talk with the teacher and was assured that henceforth the child would be allowed to go to the bathroom at her own discretion, but that seems scant satisfaction for what the child had suffered.

A writer to John Holt's *Growing Without Schooling* reported a similar incident:

> ...he urinated, or defecated, or both, in his pants. Perhaps he was ill or maybe he had a mental problem. [Author's note: Or perhaps he had merely been denied permission to go to the bathroom, which happens quite often in school.] He didn't do this regularly. He was about twelve years old. Naturally this called for punishment. He was forced to stand in front of each class in the school while the teacher explained to the class his crime. When he came to our classroom the principal named him the school's stinker and told us why. But what I remember most clearly is the pained smile on his face.[2]

The obvious conclusion in all this is simply that there are kind adults and unkind adults in schools just as there are good and bad people in every group. I think the system of school as we practice it can make good people into bad influences sometimes, but more on that later. It seems to me that an important point and possibly the main point here is that when I put my children in school, neither they nor I have much control over what adults are put in charge of them or how those adults behave. By educating my children at home, I can protect my children from emotional abuse and I make no apology for doing so.

The first year we decided to teach our children at home we visited the small town in Massachusetts where Marilyn grew up and where we met while I was stationed there in the

The Socialization Trap

Air Force. One day we were walking around town and ran into a man from our former church there who, though a generation older, had been a special friend to us. In those days we didn't know any better than to talk at leisure about our excitement about home teaching, so we shared our plans with our friend. He raised his eyebrows thoughtfully as if to say that we had an interesting idea although a bit odd. "Hmm," he said. "I guess you'd really have to be careful that the kids didn't pick up your own idiosyncracies." People use words like that in Massachusetts.

Later, as we parted company I said to Marilyn, "Just why is it that people assume our kids are going to pick up all our idio-whatever-he-said's anyway? And why are our idio-whatchacallits any worse than anybody else's for the kids to pick up?"

Having more experience now, we have learned that none of our twelve children are clones of either of us or of any of the other children. In fact, if I ever end up with a child that is exactly like one of the others, I'll take the younger one back to the hospital. There will obviously have been a mix-up in the nursery.

On the other hand, just what is so frightening about the prospect that a child might be like his parents? If God doesn't want a child to share a lot of characteristics with his parents and siblings, then the whole system of heredity is a mistake. On the contrary, I think it's good for children to spend lots of time working, playing and learning with their parents. Maybe one reason teens are sometimes uncommunicative toward their parents is that they aren't spending enough time together to keep the relationship strong. One of the reasons teenagers won't listen to their parents is that they have learned by implication that their parents are just parents and that the adults in school are the real teachers. They are the ones with the professional training and the ones who have the authority to ask questions and demand answers thirty hours a week.

This understood business of parents-aren't-teachers was brought home to me once in a conversation with a teacher whom I know personally. This lady has a master's degree in education, many years of teaching experience and is a leader in professional teachers' groups. I had asked her half jokingly why she didn't try teaching her children at home. With an uncertain chuckle she replied, "Oh, my kids won't listen to me. They'll listen to another teacher, but they won't listen to me." Apparently bent on self-destruction, I pressed the issue and suggested that perhaps if she spent thirty hours a week working with her own kids instead of somebody else's, they would listen to her (this is another one of the lessons about conversation that I hadn't learned in those early years). Another weak chuckle and she said, "Well, yeah, I guess they probably would."

Here we have one of the basic social lessons which school teaches about the adults in a child's life. Teachers are teachers and parents are parents. Parents aren't teachers. From what I've read of education in our country prior to the twentieth century, this was less of a problem in the past. When children only went to school a few months out of the year, when there was no television to further intrude between parent and child, family communication was still pretty intact. It has become evident in the last few decades that it's not only a tendency but an intention of at least the public school system in America to drive a wedge between children and their parents. The reason for this is apparent only to those who are aware that the public schools came about as means to turn our free enterprise society into a godless socialist nation. That's why it's necessary to break down the respect children have for the wisdom of their parents. Most parents are not godless or socialist in their thinking and if children listen to their parents, they will not adopt those views either. An acquaintance of mine once took a college night class and in an after-class conversation with his instructor was told the school's plan for influencing the students: "For the first two years we just work on breaking down the kids' loyalty to their parents and their religion. For the remaining two years we can teach them what we want them to know."

Which brings us back to the point that there are some bad influences among the teachers in schools. Why is it assumed that it will hurt a child to pick up his parents' individual idiosyncracies but there is no danger of them acquiring undesirable traits from school personnel? After all, a teaching job is no guarantee of good character. Today your child's teacher may be a twenty-two-year-old recent college graduate with no working experience and very little life experience. A teaching certificate can be obtained with a pretty mediocre grade point average as long as course work includes the prescribed methods courses, etc. The fact that the teacher is a pervert, irresponsible or cohabiting doesn't disqualify him or her from a teaching certificate or a teaching job. Why is that a better source of personal characteristics than most parents?

The fact that teachers are role models has no end of interesting implications. One is mentioned by James Marshall in *The Devil in the Classroom.* Commenting on teachers' strikes, Marshall says,

> ...the strike is an act of force as illegal as mugging. (Of course when teachers strike illegally it is a middle-class offense not

considered by the public as so serious as the lower-class crime of mugging). After returning to the classroom how can a striker who defies the law teach respect for law—or expect his or her authority in the classroom to be respected? Are students not given contradictory cues to legitimate behavior and conflicting values of authority?[3]

In our state it's not uncommon to see a bumper sticker that says, I CARE, THEREFORE I TEACH. I've often felt the perverse urge to print a sticker that says, "THEY CARE, THEREFORE THEY STRIKE?" If students pick up that idiosyncracy we can kiss our right-to-work laws adios.

I'm wandering here, but I can't leave this detour without sharing this little story from former Education Secretary Bill Bennett's book, *The Devaluing of America:*

> Asked "Why did the Pilgrims come to America?" an eight-year-old in New Orleans told me so that teachers could "organize and bargain collectively for wages." (Her teacher was embarrassed.)[4]

Incidentally, Bennett's book is a great read. While President Reagan's Secretary of Education, Bennett made it his practice to visit as many school classrooms around the country as he could so as to have an accurate sense of what was happening in America's schools. In reading his account of these visits, I was impressed with the difference between mediocre schools and good schools. Three underlying themes kept occurring to me as I read:

- A safe, orderly environment

- Adults who love children and challenge them to succeed

- Enthusiastic support from parents and other community adults

   While the better schools contain elements of these things,   none can match the way they operate at home.
   How do the adults in schools affect the social attitudes of children? Perhaps primarily in what they teach the child about himself. If adults treat children with respect, they will feel respectable and tend to treat others with respect. If adults make children feel important, they will have the confidence that they can succeed and so will more likely try to do so. They will also have less need to criticize or despise others in order to elevate their self esteem.
   On the other hand, if adults treat children as slaves and peons, they should expect children to rebel or lose heart and give up. It they treat them as though they had no feelings adults are obligated to respect, they should not expect inspired students who will teach themselves and be excited about plowing ahead in a given interest area beyond material covered in school. Again, a child's parents have little or no control over how their children are treated by other adults in school.
   In years past it was common for a father to tell his child that if the child got in trouble in school, he would be in bigger trouble when he got home. The insult inherent in that statement should be obvious. It assumes that the school cannot be wrong, and therefore that the child cannot be right

should he and the powers that be have a disagreement. Actually, it's an attack on the child's character and intelligence. The parent is saying, "I have so much confidence in the people at that school and so little confidence in you, that if you and they have a conflict I'll assume that you are wrong and add to whatever punishment they give you." Very encouraging. A relative of mine said of his father, "There was only one time when Dad whipped me that he shouldn't have. That time he should have gone to school and whipped the teacher." I wouldn't be surprised if that were true. And having seen the quality of some school professionals nowadays...well, never mind.

The fact is that while children in school are very dependent upon and responsible to adults, the legitimate socializing value of the contact between adult and child is virtually nonexistent. One reason is that the adults are seen by the children as role models and some are not appropriate role model material. Another reason is that the relationship is unnatural and narrow. The adult is the teacher, the child the learner. They seldom see each other outside that enviroment. Besides that, even in class there is neither time or opportunity for in-depth communication between the teacher and most of his students. One study showed that the average instructional day included 150 minutes of talking, only seven minutes of which was initiated by the students.[5]

Once I was invited to speak to a college education class about home education. A few days later I was back in the same class to observe a videotaped class debate. During the debate one of the students used something I had said to make a point. But she misquoted me as saying that I didn't think it was important for children to have personal contact with a wide variety of adults. Evidently I had failed to communicate on that point. I don't believe in home education because it keeps children away from adults other than their parents; I believe in home education (partially) because that child-adult contact is so very limited *in school*.

The way to expose children to adults socially is to get them out of the regimented isolation of school and into the real world. In school, a child has contact with only one or two adults as a rule and that contact is very limited as regards real communication. Outside school children have access to their parents, other adult relatives, neighbors and church friends. In addition, there are any number of possibilities for short-term apprenticeships that not only expose children to adults, but to the real world of work and community in which adults play their roles and for which we are supposed to be preparing our children.

Chapter 5

The System in School

What does the structure of school do for children socially? Essentially, it keeps them out of society. It isolates them in an unreal world and separates them from the real one. It teaches them to value unimportant and irrelevant things. It stifles their curiosity about life around them outside their own age group of humanity. It teaches them that some people are more valuable than others. It encourages them to be like everyone else and cast away their individuality. It makes them feel low and insignificant. It robs them of opportunities to communicate with others. The way schools are structured virtually insures that children grow up with unhealthy social attitudes.

The main reason for all this is that school in no way closely resembles the real world. The real world is a place where people of all ages live and do things together. School segregates people by age group so that the natural dynamics that build respect for the old and gentleness toward the young are not operative. Another dissimilar aspect is that in the real world people work to produce products and services to meet the needs of others. In school, people work only to learn to do the work and give other people opportunity to evaluate the work. No product, no service, no point. No satisfaction. No achievement.

School structure is good preparation for a world that doesn't exist. It teaches children that work is pointless, which it isn't. It teaches them that creativity can be turned on and off at the ringing of a bell, which it can't. It teaches them that all people should think, work and act the same, which they shouldn't.

Unfortunately, age segregation is only one of a number of unnatural forces shaping the experience of children in schools. There are a variety of factors inherent in the system as we practice it and they deserve individual attention.

One is the so-called healthy competition in academics. Children learn early in their scholastic careers that everything they do will be compared to the work done by their classmates. They are trained from the beginning to place value on a system of gold stars, percentages and grade curves that would be meaningless any place in the real world.

This healthy competition jargon is bandied about in reference to the extracurricular things too. Typical is the accepted idea that team sports are the ideal way to build a sense of teamwork. Sound familiar? "But if you home educate your children they won't be able to play team sports. They'll miss out on such good character building opportunities." Really?

In the first place, there can only be one starting quarterback. That means that teammates are adversaries automatically to a degree. For Number 2 to get a chance to play, Number 1 must be outperformed in practice. Or, if that fails to materialize, an injury could sideline Number 1 and in most cases Number 2 would find that acceptable. That is a far cry from the Biblical concept of building up one another but this is a school, not a church or a family. Another thing to be considered about school sports is that it makes enemies out of people from other schools. I think my high school experience was fairly typical in this. There were certain schools in our league who were only rivals and some who were arch-rivals. Some friends and I nearly came to serious grief one night during our senior year for no other reason than that our team won a basketball game by one point. We were saved not by the bell but by a retreat at 110 miles an hour from Newton, Kansas to Wichita.

School rivalry would seem not to be harmful if it were always kept on a friendly level. But this seems impossible. Like the old mountain family feuds, rivalries continue and intensify. One school loses a hotly contested game-perhaps because of cheating or a referee's failure-and the next year they go back looking for revenge. They now feel some strongarm tactics are justified and the other team returns the favor. A few years later the feud has developed and as in the mountain variety nobody remembers what the original offense was but only that the other people are the bad guys. We are teaching our children to see others not as individuals with needs and feelings but as members of one or another group. In other words, we are training them in ethnocentrism.

We don't need an elaborate, contrived system of gymnasiums and uniforms to teach our children cooperation and teamwork. What we need is that which is all around us: worthwhile work and healthy play with a sensitivity not to our own status but to the needs of others.

This happens better at home than anywhere else. In our own family, everyone learns that he is important. We all need each other and maybe more so than in other homes because of the number of us.   In a household of fourteen there is always a younger person needing jelly wiped off hands and face or an older somebody to look to for a push on the swing or a steadying hand on the bike. We need each other in any number of ways.   My older children help me in the family business and ministry and we all pitch in to greater and lesser degrees on the family chores—including laundry of Guiness Book proportions.

The church should be about teamwork, too. Believers are to be in the business of meeting the needs of others and of nonbelievers. If this were practiced to the intended degree I think we'd see much more spiritual fruit produced and a lot less gossip and church politics.

A simple incident taught me a lesson about teamwork that for some reason has stuck with me for years. A friend and I were demolishing an old house in exchange for as much of the lumber as we wanted. Much of the wood was in bad shape due to age, but somebody had done some recent remodeling and I came across a supporting column made of several new two-by-fours nailed together. I liked the look of these two-by-fours so I inserted the point of my pry bar in a crack between them and tried to pry them apart. Of course the post just rolled over.   I tried putting a foot on it and prying, but even my feet aren't heavy enough to withstand that much leverage. As I was looking around for some way to hold the post, Jerry saw my dilemma and before I could think to ask for a hand he walked over, stuck the point of his bar in the same crack and pried in the opposite direction. The post came apart.

In the real world, teamwork is learned differently than in the world of school. In school teamwork generally finds its expression in sports, games, spelling contests and the like. I loved all that when I was in school and I don't argue that it can be done in good friendly fun. But the fact remains that in many cases and particularly in sports, the character qualities cultivated are accompanied by an atmosphere of ethnocentrism, narcissism and status seeking.

Class distinction or social stratification is aggravated by a phenomenon referred to as labeling. Tracking—grouping children supposedly by ability—and other forms of labeling have been demonstrated to be harmful to children but the system so lends itself to them that little progress had been made toward their elimination.

The much discussed theory of learning disabilities (LD) has been very fashionable for a couple of decades now and continues to be a popular whipping boy for school failure. Dyslexia, which everybody credits and nobody understands is blamed for a multitude of reading failures even though in some countries literacy is at or near one hundred percent. One theory is that some children see the letters backwards and so reproduce them that way in writing. That stretches my gullibility a bit. Imagine an open door. The door is hinged on the left and opens toward you. Now wide open, the door is on your left and the doorway is on the right. Did you ever see a dyslexic, having reversed the door and doorway in his perception, walk into a door?

Labeling can create self-fulfilling prophecies. People have a very strong tendency to do what they are expected to do and this is exacerbated in children especially in regard to the seemingly omniscient and omnipotent adults in authority over them.

It's convenient for schools to blame mysterious maladies for academic failure, both because it removes culpability from the school and because it normally brings more money into the system as the federal government grants extra funds for each child "diagnosed" as LD. Parents are relieved too, as LD is not seen as a lack of intelligence on the part of the child, but neither as a failure on the part of the parent.

In a Wall Street Journal (I don't have the specific date) article John Gatto, 1991 New York State Teacher of the Year, gave his opinion on LD:

> David learns to read at age four; Rachel at age nine: in normal development, when both are 13, you can't tell which one learned first—the five-year spread means nothing at all. But in school I will label Rachel learning disabled and slow David down a bit too....I identify Rachel as discount merchandise, "special education." After a few months she'll be locked into her place forever.
>
> In 26 years of teaching rich kids and poor I almost never met a "learning disabled" child; hardly ever met a "gifted and talented" one, either. Like all school categories, these are sacred myths, created by the human imagination.

But many schoolists are eager to see learning disabilities and coincidentally manage to diagnose plenty of them. Estimates go as high as nearly two million students or thirty percent of all American school children. One source says:

>Many children whose intelligence is normal still have great difficulty learning to read, write or work with numbers. They see and hear perfectly well but have trouble processing what comes through the senses. As one child said, "I know it in my head, but I can't get it into my hand."[1]

I often felt that way in school. No doubt much of this is caused by throwing children into the emotional pressures of school when they are still very young and more sensitive than they will be later. Some of it is simple inexperience or immaturity misdiagnosed. When our daughter Katie was learning to write she sent my mother a letter with a small *p* or *d* made backwards. Someone who saw that immediately concluded that she was dyslexic. Katie is now eleven and she writes day and night, creating stories and dialogue that would be considered quite good even for an adult writer.

It is no less than a crime against children to teach them that they are of less quality and value than other children. Thomas Edison quit school in the elementary grades and was taught at home by his mother because the teacher had labeled him "addled." Benjamin Franklin only attended school for two years, during which time he was considered excellent in reading, fair in writing and poor in arithmetic. He taught himself and became one of the best educated and most famous men in the world. Albert Shanker, president of the American Federation of Teachers once asked a group of students who were considered at or below average the question, "What should we ask you to read?" A boy cautiously raised his hand. "Mr. Shanker," he asked, "What do the smart kids read?" He had already internalized the school's assessment that he was not one of the "smart kids."

What must this do to children? How can we expect them to enter the adult world and give it their best when we spend so many years convincing them that their best just isn't quite good enough? I heard recently about a medical test, a form of biopsy I suppose, that has been devised to test human leg muscle and determine the subject's physical capacity to develop into a championship quality distance runner. Assuming this test is medically accurate it might have some use, but one can't help wondering how many people with average muscular composition will be convinced by the biopsy that they can never be winners. Perhaps many of them possessed character qualities that would have more than compensated for their average physical potential and made them champions. So it is with school evaluations and rankings. Even if they were accurate, and I have strong doubts about that, what good are they? Supposedly they help us to group learners together by ability so we can design methodology and materials suited to their needs. Frankly, I have very little confidence in our ability to label children accurately and I'm absolutely assured that we do them much more harm than good, because the rankings convince children that their futures are less a matter of perseverance than predestination.

So we see that one reason for the self-fulfilling nature of a school label is the effect it has on the child's view of himself. But perhaps of equal or even greater importance is the label's effect on the system's opinion of him.

Speaking of economically disadvantaged children, Urie Bronfenbrenner writes:

> What social reinforcement such a child does receive in school is likely to be more contingent upon his *label* as "disadvantaged" than upon his

actual behavior. A concrete illustration of this process is useful because it highlights both a mistaken attribution of "cause" and subsequent inappropriate action which stems from this attribution. Let us consider a teacher who sees that two of her pupils are doing poorly and seeks an explanation. In her records, one of these children, Don, is labeled "disadvantaged," while the other, Albert, comes from a middle-class home. In the case of Don, she can easily *attribute* the cause of his poor performance to *him* because he has been "deprived" and cannot be expected to perform well. For Albert, however, she has no such ready explanation and hence may attribute the cause of his poor performance to her (ital) failure. As a result, she begins to react to the two boys quite differently. Albert receives more attention; Don less, since the "reasons" for his failure are "beyond her control." In due course, Albert's performance improves, while Don's deteriorates—thus validating the prior judgment of both teacher and school....In...experiments, teachers were informed that certain of their pupils could be expected to improve their academic performance substantially during the year. These children, labeled "spurters," were in fact chosen at random. The results revealed that children from whom the teachers were led to expect gains, did in fact show marked improvement, in comparison to matched controls, on objective tests of ability. The largest increments were found in the first and second grades, where the average gains in IQ were 27 and 16 points respectively.[2]

The harm in confidence, motivation and self-esteem that comes to the lower-track students is not the only damage done. The constant materialistic ranking of children is hard on the brighter students as well. A wedge is driven between children socially and it is unusual to see children mingling socially to any great degree with others in a different academic track.

As a matter of fact, children often develop an attitude of resentment toward those perceived to enjoy a favored status. Just as adults have status symbols in the form of expensive cars and houses, so do kids in their own currency. And as in the adult world, the result is sometimes class envy and resentment.

> They can treat each other with torturing cruelty. Children may reject other children because they are "too smart" or imaginative. To avoid this many youngsters try to hide their intelligence, what they read at home, and what they really think. Life among their peers may be better if they are graded B rather than the A of which they are capable.[3]

John Holt says that tracks aren't even assigned according to logical data to begin with:

> In theory, children are assigned to these tracks according to their school abilities. In practice, children are put in tracks almost as soon as they enter school, long before they have had time to show what abilities they may have. Once put in a track, few children ever escape from it. A

Chicago second grade teacher once told me that in her bottom-track class of poor nonwhite children were two or three who were exceptionally good at schoolwork. Since they learned, quickly and well, everything she was supposed to be teaching them, she gave them A's. Soon after she had submitted her first grades the principal called her in, and asked why she had given A's to some of her students. She explained these children were very bright and had done all the work. He ordered her to lower their grades, saying that if they had been capable of getting A's they wouldn't have been put in the lowest track. But, as she found upon checking, they had been put into this lowest track almost as soon as they had entered school.[4]

John Gatto relates a story from his early teaching days in which a third grade girl in a class of poor readers sailed through a selection in the reading book without a fumble. Asked why she was in the slow class, the girl replied that "they" (meaning the school authorities) had explained to her mother that she was just a bad reader with fantasies of being a good reader. Gatto invited the girl to read to him from the sixth grade book and again she performed flawlessly. This convinced the teacher that the girl was in the wrong reading class and he took her case to the principal, who responded with indignation. She told him she did not appreciate his trying to tell her how to run her school and that since he had no specialized courses in reading he should not question the judgment of the experts. Gatto persisted and the principal finally agreed to test the girl herself. A few weeks later the child stopped by Gatto's classroom to tell him that she was now in the fast class and doing very well.[5]

Along with tracking, testing is another way we classify and thus dehumanize people in school. Testing is necessary in mass education because children can't be individually evaluated just as they can't be individually instructed. And like tracking, the testing mechanism serves to rank people as having more or less of the system's approval.

Testing has some value but also has serious limitations. It measures only the material on the test itself, which is only a fraction of the material covered in class and the text materials. It certainly cannot be designed to show every thing a student knows about the subject from whatever sources he may have learned it. A skillful test taker will reflect the teacher's own opinions in essay tests and use process of elimination to increase his chances on multiple choice. Of course many factors influence test scores other than academic knowledge, for example the child's emotional condition, physical health and adequate or inadequate sleep the night before the test.

Despite the recognized limitations of tests they are still heavily relied upon in ranking students. They tell more about a student's ability to swallow and disgorge than his ability and desire to learn, yet they are used to rank children in school, gain entrance to college and place people within the armed services.

All this is sad from the viewpoint of the students who are better learners than test takers. Some students absorb well in study but are not all skillful at expressing themselves in essay questions or eliminative guessing on multiple choice or fill-in-the-blank sections.

One of the results of our penchant for testing everything children do is that they are constantly reminded of the ranking process. Those who do well on the tests get a boost to the ego but there are only ten percent of the class in the top ten percent. The other ninety percent have once again been reminded that they do not measure up-at least as far as the test is concerned. At the same time we are teaching kids to train for the test as an athlete trains for a race. The test is seen as the ultimate and logical summit of educational effort. Perhaps this is why so much of what we used to learn for tests was forgotten shortly after the test was over.

The system of schooling also teaches children passivity. A child in school is told he is there to do something but he soon learns he is there to have something done to him. He is not there to produce but to be produced. School views that child (and eventually teaches him to view himself) as a container to be filled, a trophy to be polished, a symphony to be composed. The child is the product: THE EDUCATED HUMAN BEING.

Most children aren't sure why they're in school. When I used to ask my parents why, their answer was two-fold: because the law says you have to and so you won't have to dig ditches for a living when you grow up. I wasn't crazy about the logic of either reason but I wasn't asked for my opinion . I went to school.

Kids in schools work for the sole purpose of learning how to do the work. This is in contrast to the real world where work has value because it results in products and services that meet real needs of real people. Children know that school work is a sham. They know that their work is done not because it represents supply for a need but so that someone can evaluate how well it is done. If they write a report they know it will not be read by someone who needs the information it contains but by someone whose sole purpose is to say whether it contains the information it should, and in the proper form. Every assignment is a dry run. One would think this endless tilting at windmills would drive anyone crazy, especially anyone with the creativity and curiosity of a child.

I have a friend who was a professor of education at a Christian university for many recent years. He believed in giving assignments that would cause the students to evaluate on their own what was important to learn, rather than giving them a list of his expectations for them to inhale and then exhale back to him. I once asked one of his students how she liked him as a teacher. She said that he was a very nice person, but as a teacher he made her uncomfortable because it was hard to discern "what he wanted." She had been thoroughly trained in a system in which learning was not to fulfill a perceived need on the learner's part, but rather to mechanically meet the requirements of the system and receive its artificial rewards. She didn't see that class as an opportunity to gain some useful knowledge, but as a time to discern and satisfy the teacher's desires in exchange for a favorable grade. Jump through the hoop, get the dog biscuit. Don't bother to ask why the hoop is there.

I once worked as a foreman on a construction project building college dormitories. Most of the men on my crew were college students on summer break. That summer gave me a glimpse into the minds of our modern school products. About half of the boys were good help. The other half were a study in human nature. These guys came to work, but not to work. They had no initiative and showed no interest either in learning about the work or getting any work done. They put in their hours and collected their paychecks but spent whatever time they could standing around in the unfinished dorm rooms passing the time of day. Most of them were nice kids, friendly and cheerful. But they didn't seem to connect the fact that they were at work with the idea of getting anything done. They were willing to accept their pay and it didn't seem to occur to them that the money was intended to be given in exchange for production.

I wrote all this off as youthful airheadedness, but in later years it occurred to me that this was the logical result of their training. They had spent at least twelve years doing assignments that were mere exercises and produced nothing of value to anyone else. It was no wonder that they felt they had fulfilled their obligation to the company just by being present and not making trouble. This attitude of doing just what one has to do (i.e. as little as one can get away with) is in stark contrast to the Lord's teaching in Luke 17:10 that he is an unworthy servant who does no more than is required. Such are the social values inculcated by the institution of schooling.

One of the crimes we regularly commit against children is preventing them from being needed. We are communicating to them that they need us, we don't need them. We can sequester them away from the rest of society until they are grown up, educated and hence good for something. For now, i.e., from age five to age eighteen, we will minister to their needs with high-powered techniques and technology, teaching them things they presumably couldn't learn any other way. Is it any wonder that so many adolescents are self-centered, socially myopic persons who have no direction and purpose in life? After all, they've gotten used to being done unto, not to doing.

The school system is a behemoth. More and more it is taking away the functions which God and nature intended for the family and fattening itself into a gigantic monster that dominates a child's time. We look to schools to teach children basic skills, cultural attitudes and even death education. The result is that children are so busy studying different aspects of life that they have no time to live it.

The Socialization Trap

This is partly intentional. Those who have worked in nonstandard educational systems, such as teaching illiterate adults to read, know that the amount of time spent in school is far more than what is required to learn the material taught. John Holt has found that it only takes about thirty hours for a person to learn to read if that person is ready and wants to read. John Taylor Gatto claims that plenty of evidence exists that people can learn to read, write and do basic arithmetic—in other words, learn to be self-educators—in about one hundred hours. The key, he says, is to launch out when the person expresses a desire to learn and forge ahead while the mood is still on. The regimented schedule of the average school allows for little of such individuality.

In our public schools of course, we don't do it that way. We assume all children are ready for the same learning at the same time. Never mind that little boys lag behind girls in readiness at compulsory attendance age. The fact that boys comprise eighty percent of learning disabled children and ninety percent of hyperactive children is just coincidence. Never mind that children have different interests and learning styles; just run them all through the same mill.

This approach assures enough learning problems so that there will be jobs for professionals trained to work with such problems as long as it continues. And the stretching of three to five years' worth of learning to fill twelve years of school will continue to make work for plenty of regular teachers, textbook writers, publishers and administrators.

Unfortunately, the losers in the transaction are the children who grow so institution dependent that when they do finally enter the real, adult world they are prepared to do anything but live in it.

Chapter 6

Peers in School

Institutionalists tell us that children need to go to school to have their social needs met. It is in school, they say, that children learn to get along with other people by rubbing shoulders with them day in and day out. In school, they tell us, and not sheltered at home children are able to come to grips with the real world.

The institutionalists are wrong. Age segregation is a stealthy and sinister evil that is robbing our society of its humanity. We are careful to group people with those of different sexes and races, but age isn't considered. Or rather, it is carefully considered and acted upon wrongly. As a result, we have become a fragmented society. We have a much-talked-about generation gap such as was unknown at any previous time in our history. Boy scouts were once known as little gallants who helped old ladies across the street and anybody's toddlers were everybody's pets. Now it seems old ladies dodge traffic on their own and while many people still have time to smile and admire toddlers, a woman who takes three preschoolers to the supermarket leaves others wondering just what she wants with so many little rug rats.

Perhaps the most damaging effect of age grouping in school is that it makes everybody an adversary. The constant grading and comparison never allow children to forget that they are being rated against each other. This was not true in the old one-room schoolhouse. Students in frontier schools went to school when they could and picked up where they left off. They were taught starting where they were academically, regardless of age. Some children in frontier areas didn't start school until their teenage years because there had previously been no school available. When they entered school they started at the beginning because that was the sensible place to start. A six-year-old might sit on the same bench with a fifteen-year-old and share the same spelling book.

Today's emphasis on mass production lumps children together by birth year. This, of course, defies the findings of research that children differ in ability and readiness, that boys generally lag behind girls in maturity during the early years, etc. It should come as no surprise that eighty percent of "learning disabled" children are boys as are ninety percent of "hyperactive" children. But schools already have their

77

minds made up; they can't be distracted by the facts. It is convenient to group kids by age and so we do.

As a child looks around for the first time at a room full of children his own age, he begins to develop a new view of the world. He now learns that he is bigger than some children his age and smaller than others. He is heavier or lighter, taller or shorter. He runs faster or slower and learns some things faster or more slowly as well. It begins to sink in that he has a ranking among his fellows whereas before he didn't know such a ranking existed. Soon he discovers tests and grades and learns that the authorities are consciously ranking him as he is beginning to rank himself. Others around him are ranking him too and he begins to rank them.

Now a pattern has emerged and the child watches it grow. He is learning that success has less to do with the quality of his work as compared to the need it meets—it meets no need that he can see—than with the quality of his work as compared to the work of others. Once he realizes this every other child in the room becomes a threat. Because he is now being graded on a curve, compared with his peers, success now is a matter of doing better than someone else. His success requires that others fail. This is why such petty rivalries arise in school classrooms. It is also a reason for the constant pressure and tension many children feel and the eagerness with which children point out flaws in the work and behavior of others. A child soon learns that making some one else look worse makes him look better.

This unceasing competition and comparison is supposed to be good for children, hence the phrase "healthy competition." It's not uncommon for adults to view school competition as necessary. After all, they say, they'll have to compete for jobs some day. Let 'em learn what it's like now.

The Socialization Trap

That doesn't hold water in a Biblical world view.
Christians are to look to God, not their employers, for
provision. Besides, we believe that God has a plan for each
of our lives. If that's true, we should have no fear of
someone else getting a job we want. God is in control of
that.

But few of us have a Biblical world view. And this age-
peer upbringing is part of the reason. As we build in our
children, mostly by implication, the assumption that
everybody is to be graded and ranked among his peers we are
teaching them that some people are more and less valuable
than others. Once that preconception takes root, a godly
frame of reference goes out the window. The child learns to
see himself not as a unique creation of a loving Maker but a
mark on a numbered scale.

The tendency of school peer groups toward the
establishment of a pecking order is illustrated by a childhood
experience John Holt relates:

> ...When I was nine, I was in a public
> elementary school, in a class in which almost all
> the boys were bigger and older than I was...One
> by one, the toughest ones first, then the others,
> more less in order of toughness, they beat me up
> at recess, punched me until they knocked me
> down and/or made me cry. Once a boy had
> beaten me up, he rarely bothered to do it again.
> There didn't seem to be much malice in it; it was
> as if this had to be done in order to find my proper
> place in the class. Finally everyone had beat me
> except a boy named Henry. One day the bigger
> boys hemmed us in and told us that we had to
> fight to find who was the biggest sissy in the sixth

grade. Henry and I said we didn't want to fight. They said if we didn't, they would beat up both of us. So for a while Henry and I circled around, swinging wildly at each other, the bigger boys laughing and urging us on. Nothing happened for some time, until one of my wild swings hit Henry's nose. It began to bleed, Henry began to cry, and so did I. But the bigger boys were satisfied; they declared that Henry was now the official biggest sissy in the class.[1]

I can recall many times throughout my years of schooling when the same sort of thing happened, although I never noticed the pecking order so clearly outlined as in the above quote from Holt. An element that did strike me as consistent, though, was the eagerness with which more powerful boys used to greet an opportunity to harass or intimidate another boy. Being one of the smallest boys in a class of around two hundred children, I came in for my share of this sadistic treatment. I'm satisfied that if all adults could clearly remember their own times of intimidation in school, many more people would be teaching at home.

A pattern that repeated itself all through my high school career was the harassment of freshmen by sophomores. It was clearly traditional that freshmen boys were fair game for any kind of intimidation, harassment and even downright cruelty. The interesting thing about it was that the great majority of the hazing came from sophomores. Juniors and seniors picked on freshmen occasionally, but the sophomores seemed to be on the lookout constantly for an opportunity to hassle a freshman. It seemed to be an unwritten rule that they had taken their lumps the previous year and they now had the right to give the same treatment to others. I suspect there was a heavy dose of security-seeking in all this; the sophomores seemed not just eager but driven to the behavior. It was as if they needed to assure themselves that they were no longer the lowest creatures in the pecking order; there was someone weaker and more defenseless than they were.

It is not only in aggression, but also in a number of other negative forms of behavior that the influence of the peer group in school makes itself known:

The "peer groups" into which we force children have many other powerful and harmful effects. Every now and then, in the subway or some public place, I see young people, perhaps twelve or thirteen years old, sometimes even as young as ten, smoking cigarettes...The smoke tastes awful...They have to struggle not to choke, not to cough...Why do they do it? Because "all the other kids" are doing it, or soon will be, and they have to stay ahead of them, or at least not fall behind. In short, wanting to smoke, or feeling one has to smoke whether one wants to or not, is one of the many fringe benefits of that great "social life" at school that people talk about.

...If the children have lived in the peer group long enough to become enslaved to it, addicted to it—we might call them peer group junkies—then they are going to smoke, and do anything and everything else the peer group does. If Mom and Pop make a fuss, then they will lie about it and do it behind their backs. The evidence on this is clear. In some age groups, fewer people are smoking. But more children are smoking every year, especially girls, and they start earlier.

...Of course, children who spend almost all
their time in groups of other people their own age,
shut out of society's serious work and concerns,
with almost no contact with any adults except
child-watchers, are going to feel that what "all the
other kids" are doing is the right, the best, the only
thing to do.[2]

Just today, Marilyn and I stood at our kitchen window
and watched some of our children playing in our back yard
and garden area. Our children are expert dirt sculptors and
have created some pretty intricate communities of buildings
and roads. What we saw as we watched would have looked
very strange to a lot of people. We had four little girls
playing in the sandbox and out beyond the garden, dirt
creations were being developed by our eight-year-old
daughter and two of her teenage brothers. I couldn't help
remarking to Marilyn how the boys would be ostracized if
they were in school and some classmate of theirs should see
them doing something considered so infantile, and alongside
their eight-year-old sister at that. But our boys think nothing
of it because they don't care that it's not socially acceptable.
To them it's no more infantile to create communities in dirt
than it is to an engineer to create them on paper.

Our children are, in my opinion, refreshingly different in
this. They do what they like to do and what they need to do,
without the emotional albatross of worrying about what is
socially acceptable. Our kids don't care that one brand of
blue jeans is more stylish than another; brand names are
meaningless to them in any kind of clothing. They don't feel
obligated to know what musical groups are in vogue (thanks
be to God), the current teen lingo, or the other trappings of
peer group addiction.

The Socialization Trap

At the same time some of our kids' behavior would impress their peers as infantile, they demonstrate in other ways unusual maturity. From the age of fifteen and on up, all our sons are currently working full time in our family construction business. They do a man's work and do it well and have developed quite a reputation within the rough fraternity of tradesmen. They also pitch in and take part in caring for the younger children, the ideal training for future parents. The older boys are also regularly called upon for help when the church needs hands moving chairs and tables for a dinner or there is some repair work to be done. Seventeen-year-old Tim sometimes plays piano preludes and offertories for services, as does eight-year-old Emily. Marilyn and I shake our heads when we think about how we grew up and compare that to the freedom our children have to mature in different areas at their own pace and in their own way. That liberty would be impossible if they were addicted to the approval of an age peer group.

Chapter 7

Curriculum

You're probably already acquainted with the battle of the books. Starting with Mel and Norma Gabler in Texas in the early 1960's, parents' groups have made national headlines with their protests of the garbage in public school texts. Humanism, socialism, moral perversion and the occult now thoroughly permeate the materials in the public schools and some private schools as well.

Why should we as home educators be concerned about the texts in the government schools? After all, those schools don't have our children. Actually, there are several good reasons to be concerned and if God leads, involved in the fight.

One good reason is that you and I are paying for those books. As of this writing public education is costing

$6,300.00 per year for each student. A large part of that money goes for materials, including text books. And the money is coming out of the pockets of tax payers.

Another reason is that some Christian schools are using some of the same textbooks as the public schools. Of course, no responsible Christian school would use books full of profanity or anti-American dogma, but there is a significant amount of objectionable material in many books that is cleverly hidden among acceptable subject matter and it's not always easily detected. Just a few years ago national attention focused on some contested books in Tennessee schools and the court case became known as the Scopes II trial. Shortly after the case hit the headlines it was discovered that some of the books in question were being used in a large and well-known Christian school not far from where we live. If we care about our brethren who choose Christian school over home education we need to be concerned about textbooks.

At the same time, we as Christians have a responsibility to be interested in the welfare of everyone in the community and that includes the children in the public schools. Most of their parents are not informed about the dangers hidden in curriculum materials. Just as it was Christians who led society in the fight to free the slaves and end exploitive child labor, it should now be Christians who make up the vanguard in the battle of the books.

Perhaps the weightiest reason that we should be interested in this subject is that these books do, in the end, have an effect on the lives of our children. How so? In that our kids will have to share a world with the products of the government school system. They will have to live in the same neighborhoods with people who have been taught there is no absolute right and wrong, vote against people who believe that freedom is no better than statism and rear children in a society in which venereal disease, crime and family disintegration are the order of the day. Around eighty percent of American children still attend public school and so we can expect our society to be saturated with the values and opinions prevalent there. The outcome will be the nation we leave to our children.

Here are some of the lies being foisted upon innocent children by textbooks in various subjects:

Values Education: There is no right or wrong. You have the right to set your own moral standards.

History: The founders of this nation were not particularly special. Their wisdom and religious beliefs are not significant. Most of them were Deists. By the way, patriotism is outmoded.

Science: Man descended from monkeys. You are just another animal and your existence is an accident.

Economics: Socialism may be expected to sweep the globe because its superiority over capitalism is being recognized. Capitalism causes greed and is inherently evil.

Government: Big government is responsible to meet everyone's needs. Free enterprise is not to be trusted and individual initiative is unimportant.

Although not necessarily in order, this chapter will discuss these subjects and others in which objectionable text materials are being used to secularize and pervert children.

To Read or Not to Read

Before we get into the use of textbooks and other curriculum materials intended to mold the social values, we should at least mention the controversy over phonics versus sight word reading instruction. This fight has been raging for decades with countercharges between proponents of the two systems flying left and right. As early as 1929 articles began appearing in professional journals commenting on this conflict.

According to education commentator Sam Blumenfeld, there are now more than 24 million functional illiterates in the United States. A functional illiterate is not one who has had no instruction in reading but rather a person who has had reading instruction but reads so poorly that he cannot function effectively in the basic responsibilities for which reading should equip a person such as taking a driver's test or filling out a job application. Blumenfeld attributes this to the use of look-say or sight word reading instruction in the public schools rather than an emphasis on phonics.

Briefly, the idea of sight word reading comes from the ideographic approach to language. In Chinese for example, symbols in the alphabet stand for ideas rather than for sounds as in our alphabetic system. Thus there is a symbol for dog that could be read dog, puppy, or canine—different words with different meanings and sounds. Ideographic languages require many more symbols because a symbol is needed for every word, whereas we can spell any word in our language with an alphabet of only twenty-six letters. Blumenfeld says that there is a Chinese typewriter in the United Nations building that has 5,000 keys.

Sight word reading was first introduced by Professor Gallaudet, a teacher of deaf students. He found that while deaf children could not associate letters with sounds, they could memorize the shape and placement of letters in groups. He was able to help his students memorize some words in this way and so was able to teach them to read to some extent. The limitation of this system was that because letters do not have shapes that look like the idea they represent (for instance, the three letters of the word dog do not look like a picture or outline of a dog) the whole system depended on rote memory and so was limited to a comparatively small number of words that could be memorized.

The early proponents of public education learned of Professor Gallaudet's system and determined to try it as they had noticed that most children could in fact recognize some whole words before they had learned the alphabet. So as early as the 1830's the fledgling public school system in Massachusetts began experimenting with look-say reading.

The limitations of the method soon became apparent. By the second or third grades children taught to read by sight word were significantly behind students learning traditional phonics. This caused the private school teachers to rise up in alarm and call attention to the problem. Soon sight word reading was in public disrepute, but Horace Mann and the other social engineers who were pushing for universal public and compulsory schooling kept it alive in their neophyte Normal Schools (later called teacher's colleges) and it made a comeback in the early 1900's. At that time John Dewey, the socialist philosopher and educator picked up the idea and along with others, maneuvered its widespread acceptance in the public schools, which by then had spread to every state and educated a far higher percentage of American students than in Mann's day.

Dewey's philosophy maintained that people were too individualistic and selfish and needed to be guided toward a more altruistic or "social" attitude toward life. He suggested a departure form the ancient tradition of concentrating on literacy in the first two years of school and substituting an emphasis on social skills and experiential learning instead. He knew that sight word readers did not read as well as children who were taught phonics, but literacy was not as important as social attitudes in his economy, and he was confident that his students would catch up on reading and writing in the higher grades. It later became apparent that this was in fact not happening, but Dewey and the other "progressive'" educators were not concerned. In fact, this rather suited their social goals because those who read well and widely tend to learn to think independently and critically. This would not do in the statist, socialist nation they had envisioned.

This puts me in mind of the fact that prior to the Civil War in this country, it was illegal to teach a slave to read. The reason, of course, was that people who learn to read and read widely are poor prospects for slaves. That is a good commentary on Dewey and the legacy he left us in the government schools.

Blumenfeld points out that both the Protestant Reformation and the American War of Independence (it was not a revolution) would have been impossible without widespread literacy, for that very reason. John Gatto has stated that Thomas Paine's *Common Sense* sold 600,000 copies to an American population of only 3 million when one in five of those were slaves and fully one half indentured servants. The idea of widespread American literacy that this suggests is confirmed by studies such as those done by Professor Lawrence Cremin, which show literacy in America to be near one hundred percent of the non-slave population by the time we gained our independence. Blumenfeld quotes a 1915 publication in which US Bureau of Education statistics showed that in the year 1910 only one child in a thousand in Massachusetts between the ages of ten and fourteen was illiterate. Then he quotes a Boston Globe editorial written in 1984 that states, "about 40 percent of the city's adult population is believed to be functionally illiterate." "What a staggering difference" Blumenfeld says, "and at a time when 'science' is supposed to have taught us more about education than our highly literate ancestors ever knew!"[1]

The cornucopia of reading problems which sight word reading instruction has brought about has been a boon to the public education establishment. It has created jobs for thousands of remedial reading specialists and others, and at the same time contributed to the spawning of generations of Americans who cannot read or think critically and depend on television with its obvious liberal bias for their opinions and values, thus paving the way for the steady encroachment of socialism to which Mann, Dewey and many others devoted their lives.

What does all this have to do with our discussion of socialization? In a nutshell, I'm saying that people who learn to read phonetically are usually better readers than those taught by look-say. Better readers are better thinkers, generally speaking. Better thinkers are harder to convince of socialist dogmas such as the idea that politicians know better what are the needs of the common man than he himself does.

Those who read and think independently question illogical statements. They are able to read the Scriptures and contrast its teachings on private property and local provision for the poor with the Big Brother philosophy of social programs advanced by the statists. They can understand that moral questions do indeed have absolute answers, that abstinence is the solution to sexually transmitted disease, that free enterprise is more logical than collectivism and that individuals are responsible for their own actions rather than their environment. In short, literate people are more capable than illiterate people of developing a philosophy of life that results in healthy relationships with the other people in their world.

A functionally illiterate populace fits beautifully with the goals of those who would turn America in to a socialist state dominated by a powerful central government. As long as people sit mesmerized in front of televisions and swallow the picture of the world given to them by the liberal news media instead of reading widely and forming their own opinions, the socialist agenda will march on. Swallowers are followers, readers are leaders.

Secularization

Another modern educational phenomenon that dovetails with the socialist purpose in schooling is the removal of religion from the curriculum. While I would be the first to assign responsibility for a child's religious education to his parents, the fact is that public education today is making every effort to secularize children by denying the dominant role religion has played in our history and still plays in our society. It's not hard to see why this is done; a society with a healthy fear of God will produce people who stop and think

91

about right and wrong and whether there might not be prescribed ways of conducting social life.

This denial of the importance of religion, particularly Christianity, is not passive but very active. A pastor friend of mine defended his child's attendance at public school by asserting that he could teach his daughter the things of God at home. He needed, he said, no help from the school. That's very true but entirely beside the point. If the school were only neglectful toward Christianity as he seems to think, there would be little problem. He could, indeed, give his daughter her Christian training at home. But the sad fact is that the public schools are doing all they can not just to leave the subject alone but to tear Christian principles down at every opportunity. Children are encouraged to celebrate Halloween in school, but not Christmas or Easter. The school break for the Christmas season is now officially referred to as "winter holidays" instead of "Christmas vacation." When I was a boy, the Gideons came to the school every year giving away new Testaments to the children. Now they have to work the sidewalks in front to the school. Prayer is forbidden in graduation exercises if sponsored by the school.

Besides the fact that the school system has taken an official stance against Christianity, the simple absence of the Bible from science, history and psychology courses automatically skews a student's view of the subject matter. When a book or course presents an important subject without mention of God it is saying to the student that God is not important to the understanding of the subject. If you'll think about this a minute you'll realize how true this is. Children in school learn by implication that the school, teachers and textbooks are omniscient and they really do tend to assume that what is not contained in the course is not critical to the topic. It is tragic today that most Christians (let alone the general public) don't know how providentially our country was protected as it fought for its independence or how George Washington, Abraham Lincoln and other great Americans depended upon God for guidance when the nation's needs were greatest. I graduated from high school with no awareness of the Great Awakening or the revivals that swept the country before and during the Civil War. I heard much about FDR but nothing about Charles Finney. Though in the very early years some lip service had been given to the fact that the Pilgrims had come to the New World for religious freedom, by the time I graduated I had a secularized view of history. And I graduated almost twenty-five years ago. It is much worse now.

Former education secretary Bill Bennett speaks to this secularization of education in *The Devaluing of America:*

> "What the American people don't understand... and I think they are right not to understand it, is that a group of students, can, by law, get together and say, 'We must all advance the Marxist revolution.' A group of students can get together and say, 'I don't like reds, I like green drugs. What kind of drugs do you like?' A group of students can get together and talk about various methods of birth control. But they can't get together and say, 'Our Father, Who art in heaven, hallowed be Thy name.'"
>
> In too many places in American public education, religion has been ignored, banned, or shunned in ways that serve neither knowledge, nor the Constitution, nor sound public policy. There is no good curricular or constitutional

reason for text books to ignore, as many do, the role of religion in the founding of this country or its prominent place in the lives of many of its citizens. We should acknowledge that religion—from the Pilgrims to the civil rights struggle—is an important part of our history, civics, literature, art, music, poetry, and politics, and we should insist that our schools tell the truth about it. As I told the American Jewish Committee, "there is a confusion among some teachers and some principals that, because the schools should not be used to encourage people to be members of one religious faith or another...the whole question of religion in our society is out of bounds. That," I said, "is wrongheaded and silly."

If students are learning about Western art, how are they to understand the paintings of Michelangelo, Raphael, or Fra Angelicao, which depict religious figures and events?

The extremes to which some will go to deny the place of religion in American life is mind-boggling. A 1986 study by New York University professor Paul Vitz, for instance, found that the overwhelming majority of elementary and high school textbooks go to extraordinary lengths to avoid *any* references to religion. One sixth grade reader, for example, includes a story called, "Zlateh the Goat," by the late Novel Laureate Isaac Bashevis Singer. In Singer's story, a boy named Aaron is told to take Zlateh, the family goat, to a butcher in the next village to be sold. On the way, Aaron and Zlateh get caught in a three-day blizzard and are lost in the snow. At this point, Singer writes, "Aaron began to pray to God for himself and for the innocent animal." But in the school reader this has been changed to: "Aaron began to pray for himself and for the innocent animal." Later, after Aaron and Zlateh have found shelter in a haystack, Singer writes, "Thank God that in the hay it was not cold." But in the reader this had been changed to: "Thank goodness that in the hay it was not cold."

"This would be funny if it were not so serious," I said in a 1986 speech. "Has the very mention of God's name in public become an offense?"[2]

Again the question comes to mind of what all this has to do with the children of home educators and children in private schools. The answer is that first of all, the vast majority of children in this country are still in public schools. They will have a drastic effect on the future of the country. Further, many teachers in Christian schools have been educated in public schools and even in secular colleges and so will bring some secular influence into the Christian schools. As I stated earlier, many Christian schools use secular texts. The potential effects of that should be evident. The combination of all these factors make it obvious that the only way to give our children a truly Christian education that will help them shine as lights in the darkness and have a part in turning our ever more secular society back to God is to teach them at home and use materials that give God His rightful place.

An illustration of the secularization of history comes from the World Book Encyclopedia. I have a set of these and I looked up Lincoln's Gettysburg address after having read that the words, "under God" were omitted from the famous speech in most history texts. I was irritated and fascinated with what I found. The encyclopedia entry quotes the entire speech (supposedly). Reading the last few lines I saw an interesting thing. The text read, "...that we here highly resolve that these dead shall not have died in vain; that this nation shall have a new birth of freedom..." A picture above the column shows the text of the speech engraved in stone in the Lincoln monument and it is clearly visible that it reads, "that we here highly resolve that these dead shall not have died in vain; that this nation UNDER GOD (emphasis mine) shall have a new birth of freedom..." Historical revisionism in an encyclopedia and the proof of its falsehood barely three inches away! (Note: my edition of this encyclopedia was published in 1960. A reader has written since the first printing of this book to let me know that in her 1988 edition of *World Book*, the words "under God" appear where they should in the text. I don't know the explanation.)

This brings us to the Gablers. Mel and Norma Gabler are a couple in Longwood, Texas who noticed this same deletion in their son's high school history text in the early 1960's. This discrepancy cued them to the degeneration of school texts and the creeping influence of humanism in school. The Gablers quickly became alarmed at how pervasive the corruption had become and before long were testifying in hearings about what they saw as wrong. Soon they were in contact with parents and other concerned citizens across the country who were beginning to see problems as well. Today the Gablers are nationally known textbook critics and their names are generally seen in news articles wherever parents are publicly objecting to bad textbooks.

The Socialization Trap

Who's Calling the Shots?

In their 1985 book, *What Are They Teaching Our Children?* the Gablers answer the question, "What are the issues at stake?" Their answer: Do parents have the primary right—preeminent over the school and state—to control the education of the children? Or do educators—who hold values that differ from parents—have the right to determine the spiritual, political, and economic outlook of students?

> Should schools teach knowledge, skills, and the heritage of the home, church, and nation? Or should they teach students that knowledge is what is personally "relevant" to them? Do educators have the right to use our children as guinea pigs in behavior modification experiments? Should our children be under the direction of idealogues hostile to Judeo-Christian values and American Constitutional liberty?
>
> The basic issue is simple: Which principles will shape the minds of our children? Those which uphold family, morality, freedom, individuality and free enterprise; or those which advocate atheism, evolution, secularism, and a collectivism in which an elite governs and regulates religion, parenthood, education, property, and the lifestyle of all members of society?[3]

The authors then go on to make a very credible case in the remainder of the book that the above process is indeed well under way in the public schools and their texts. I strongly recommend the Gablers' book.

This may be an illogical juncture at which to do this, but having just finished skimming their excellent book I feel a compulsion to comment on one point. Mel and Norma Gabler have done the Lord and our society an invaluable service by exposing the garbage in the public school texts. With that as a jumping off point, let me comment that I feel we need to act on their lead and in fact take the process of purification farther. Christians everywhere in America are up in arms against what is going on in the public schools. The great truth we are overlooking is that correcting the problems in the government schools would in fact require eliminating the whole school system. The government, and more specifically the NEA lobbyists who control public education, have achieved a fraudulent monopoly on the education business in the United States. As Sam Blumenfeld and others have documented, the public education system was never needed in the first place and came into existence only because Horace Mann and his cohorts wanted to change our democracy into a socialistic, humanistic society. Before nationwide public schooling the educational needs of the nation were very adequately met by home education, proprietary schools, church schools, charity schools, apprenticeships and combinations of these. Education was better then and not incidentally our social problems were drastically less severe.

Horace Mann and his Unitarian friends wanted to eliminate the teaching of the depravity of man and original sin. Robert Owen and his followers wanted to eliminate free enterprise (capitalism) and the selfishness which they thought resulted from it. As these two groups began to work together and lure well-meaning but deluded humanitarians into the movement with them, they created, first through the Massachusetts legislature and then in other states, state boards of education governing and expanding the public or "common" schools which had until then been under primarily local control. Horace Mann became the first state Secretary of Education in 1837. Twenty years later, the organization that would one day be known as the National Education Association was formed. In 1976, Jimmy Carter was elected president of the United States and moved with due expediency to take education out of the purview of the Department of Health, Education and Welfare, honoring a promise made in exchange for the support of the NEA in his campaign. Now the liberals had a national system of education and a cabinet-level secretary to head it up without interference from those concerned with other things than schooling. Their power was greatly increased.

The logical conclusion of this leftward-leaning process is now plainly visible. As the Gablers have discovered in textbooks, the philosophy of the public schools is now unabashedly one of virtually undiluted humanism, socialism, amorality, situational ethics, and irresponsible sexuality and rebellion to authority. The question which must be addressed is not *how* it should be reformed but *whether* it should be reformed. My answer to the second question is no, it should not be reformed; it should never have been formed the first time. But that is too idealistic. The fact is that most American children attend public school and if the schools are not reformed the children will continue to be hurt as badly as now. The school system will not die and release its victims suddenly.

Part of the answer is already being given: Get kids out of those schools. As the decade of the seventies turned into the decade of the eighties, private schools were starting in this country at the rate of one every seven hours. More recently home education has become a tidal wave which eventually will sweep the country. I believe home education is the Scriptural, normal and natural way for children to get their basic education. But there will always be a need for alternatives of some kind because some people will not choose to teach their own children. Private schools are acceptable alternatives; public schools are not. Public, government funded education has, throughout history, been used as a tool of indoctrination and enslavement of citizens by their leaders. Schools must always be under the control of the parents of the students through the right of parents to place their children in the system of their choice. This is why some system of school choice is essential and will, I suspect, eventually be demanded by the populace of this country. There is the potential of government control in a voucher system, but ways can and must be found to give parents back some of the $6300.00 in tax money it is now (1993) costing to "educate" a child in the government system, and give it back without strings attached.

I'd like to make some simple recommendations for Christian parents concerned about the situation in our schools:

1. Take your children out of school and teach them at home. This is the only way you can have final control over what they read, the values they assimilate and the influences to which they are exposed. Private Christian school is an alternative for those who absolutely cannot teach at home.

2. Support the establishment of private schools. As their superiority over the public schools gains more public awareness the hold of the government on education will

weaken and influence will return to the local people who share the values espoused by the God-fearing founders of this country.

3. As God leads, be a part of the movement to call attention to the flaws in public education. This is not to attack the character of the many sincere people who teach in those schools because they love children and like teaching, but rather to call into account the moral and philosophical rot that has set in and the bureaucratic control that has taken place of local sentiment in determining what goes on in the classroom.

The only sensible goal for the public education system is its eventual elimination. It never should have existed, it has only brought educational damage and it should not be allowed to perpetuate its destruction only because it has powerful allies in government. It will not happen overnight but it can be done and when it does America will be a cleaner, healthier place where democracy and Christian principles can once again bring the blessings of freedom to the millions who have forgotten what it's like.

Other Forms of Brainwashing

Values Clarification: Probably the area most often disputed in public discussion on textbooks is the topic of *moral values education* (MVE). Usually referred to by the name of its most common form, Values Clarification, this topic has made headlines repeatedly and raised blood pressure levels for several different groups of people involved. Parents have been up in arms (as well they should) when their children come home and share some of the things they are learning. The result has been that in some places the objectionable texts have been removed from the school system. But the latter condition of things may be more dangerous than before because the humanists, finding tough sledding in using their materials as they were originally introduced, have found ways of mixing poison in the punch so that it is harder to detect and eliminate.

What is values clarification? Evidently a direct descendant of Joseph Fletcher's philosophy of situational ethics, this program teaches simply that there is no absolute right or wrong. Children are invited to form their own values. The approach is insidious in that while claiming to teach no standards or assumptions, it contains standards that are based on assumptions. Children are given hypothetical problems and asked what they would do in if they were actually in the situation. Often use is made of role playing to make it more realistic.

When I worked for the Virginia prison system I was required to take a five-week training course which included a segment called Human Relations. Part of this segment involved hypothetical situation resolution which plainly reflected values clarification techniques. By this I know that values clarification had found its way into the training of government employees as early as the mid-1970's.

One situation we discussed was the now-familiar fallout shelter scenario. There are nine people in the shelter and only enough food, water and air for eight to survive. We were given information about the occupants and asked which ones should be allowed to stay inside (this was more polite than asking which one should be thrown out for destruction.) As the group talked, consideration was given to age, health, gender, education, etc. The idea was to select for liquidation the one deemed least necessary to the preservation of species and society after the holocaust. We went around the circle in our thoughtful little discussion group sharing sagely practical opinions until it was my turn to speak. I told them that my verdict was that I would have no part of making such decision. I had no right, I explained, to make decisions that are not under man's domain. The instructor, in true non-judgmental style, told the group that my decision was valid and we moved on around the circle.

It would have been interesting had someone brought up the question of whether additional supplies could have been found to support an extra life, or if there might be another bomb shelter nearby with space available. But such considerations are not included in the problem. And why not? Because the creators of values clarification are not interested in helping a student *clarify* what he believes, but in influencing him to *change* what he believes. Hence the hypothetical situations (usually very unlikely scenarios) don't include a lot of flexibility to provide escape routes. The intention is to force the participants to choose from a very limited number of options so that they will have to act under the assumption that they have the right to choose between the options given. This is the "value" they want to "clarify."

Another common problem used in values clarification exercises is the Life Raft scenario. In Dr. Kathleen M. Gow's book, *Yes, Virginia, There Is Right and Wrong* she quotes an article from the *Catholic Register:*

> Ten students were placed on a "raft" in a swimming pool and asked to act out the dilemma. After some discussion, the students decided which two among them were least worthy to remain in the raft. Then they grabbed these two, fully

clothed, and tossed them into the pool. One of the boys ejected was colored; the other was an epileptic who had been in a special education class. The mother of the epileptic told the *Register* she was "terribly upset" by the incident. "The principal didn't even want to talk to me about it. I asked him: Suppose my son had a seizure?"[4]

Here we have a prime example of godless socialization. Children are put in a situation where they are actually capable of throwing others into a swimming pool and do so. A nonwhite child and a mentally handicapped child are the victims. One of the two could have had an epileptic seizure and drowned. But the principal doesn't feel obligated even to discuss it with the mother of the boy. There is certainly values education going on here. But what values are being inculcated?

One mother whose daughter was involved in the life raft exercise wrote, "I was shocked to find that her group was the only group out of four that solved the life raft problem by having the strongest swimmers take turns swimming along with the raft, therefore avoiding throwing someone overboard to die. These children were made to feel that this was not a solution that was acceptable, because they were asked to choose whom they would throw over, not whether they would. I complained to the teacher and was told 'not to be so upset, it was only a hypothetical problem.'" This happened in a private religious school.[5]

Children are being taught that they have the right to democratically decide who is worthy to live and who is not. Perhaps it is representative of the larger society in which we live that it was the "defective" person and the member of the minority group who were selected for elimination. This is just the sort of thing taking place now in real life through abortion, infanticide and euthanasia. The schools are a primary agent in the fostering of these godless, materialistic social attitudes. Yet home educators are criticized for the "unhealthy" socialization of their children.

Values educators often put children through short-answer exercises as well. In this method, students are asked to rank choices in a better-or-worse format. For instance, the assignment is to rank stealing from a department store, stealing from a class bully, stealing from a rich person and stealing from a blind man. Which is the worse offense from the student's point of view? Again, it is strongly implied that the children have the authority ("We shall be as gods") to assign such rankings. It is also assumed—both by the curriculum and the participants—that there is such a thing as better and worse theft. Stealing might not be so bad; it depends on from whom you steal.

Death Education: Would you like for your son or daughter to be taught how to commit suicide? Such instruction is available in many curricula. Along with values education, death education is now helping children to "clarify" (read 'modify') their attitudes toward living and dying. Dr. Gow writes about a fifth grade teacher who took his class through a three-day course on death and dying. It's pretty sickening, but I include some notes about it so you can get a glimpse of what your home-taught child is missing.

Day One: Students took their choice of these topics for extra-credit reports: Mummies, pyres, cremation, embalming, and stone for graves. For spelling, words such as undertaker, morgue, mourn, bury etc. were used. Math class consisted of funeral-related problems. For discussion, the class listed ways to die and the related advantages and disadvantages of each.

Day Two: The pupils wrote a story using some of their spelling words. The title was, "*How I Died.*" They watched a filmstrip called, "*Facts about Funerals.*" Discussion time centered on death-related idioms such as: over my dead body, starving to death, etc. For math, the children measured their own coffins in English and metric units. In social studies (don't you love that term) the students were assigned role playing, with three of the seven groups acting out death-related scenes.

Day Three: The children were blessed with a guest speaker, a funeral director brought in to discuss funerals and answer the children's questions about death and dying. No doubt an in-depth look at a grave subject (okay, okay, I admit it's not funny). Class discussion dealt with questions: What would you die for? etc. In language class, students chose two of these three activities: Write your own obituary, write your own will, draw your own tombstone.[6]

Pardon me. I never finished college and no doubt my understanding is lacking, but would someone explain to me why all (or for that matter, any) of this voodoo education is necessary? What do fifth grade children need with a three-day course in such lunacy as writing their own obituaries? This massive overkill on a subject with which most ten-year-olds have very little experience is a macabre but typical example of schooling run amok. Children need to learn about death sometime, but it should take place in a manner and at a time when the child's parents deem appropriate. One has to wonder whether the parents of the fifth graders who suffered this emotional abuse were informed of what was about to happen beforehand. Would any loving parent submit his child to such a thing? This exercise was clearly outrageous. The whole thing took place in a strictly secularized frame of reference, it was perpetrated on people far too young and it was given a degree of intensity that could only have damaged the children. Another teacher, taking exception to the three-day deathfest, wrote that her own school district had been successfully sued by the parents of a 13-year-old girl who had taken part in a similar project and had developed an obsessive fear of death. Interestingly, *decreasing* the fear of death is one of the goals of death education. Dr. Gow quotes a study showing that in fact such courses *increase* this fear in children, and the students studied were tenth graders—five years older than the fifth graders in the three-day course.

The Gablers have recorded some similar documentation and they have unearthed some interesting data on other facets of curricula as well:

Secular Humanism: The Supreme Court has declared that Secular Humanism is a religion. Yet while Christianity is banned for the public classroom Humanism is rampant. The Gablers quote *The Humanist* magazine:

> "The battle for humankind's future must be waged and won in the public school classroom by teachers who correctly perceive their role as the proselytizers of a new faith: a spark of what theologians call divinity in every human being. These teachers must embody the same selfless dedication as the most rabid fundamentalist preachers, for they will be ministers of another sort, utilizing a classroom instead of a pulpit to convey humanist values in whatever subject they teach, regardless of the educational level—

preschool, day care, or large state university. The classroom must and will become an arena of conflict between the old and the new—the rotting corpse of Christianity...and the new faith of humanism..." [7]

Humanists are not only ambivalent toward Christianity; they are devotedly opposed to it. They will use occultish Halloween motifs in the classroom and some schools actually make *Dungeons and Dragons* available to students. One middle school, say the Gablers, offered *D&D* as an elective.[8] Of course the Bible is still available to most American children, so the Humanists substitute dilution for elimination. Mel and Norma quote from a textbook dealing with mythology and "explaining" the crossing of the Red Sea by the Israelites fleeing Egypt by saying that the sea was in fact only six inches deep at the crossing point. I wonder if they've ever come up with an answer for the old riddle as to how Pharaoh's whole army drowned in six inches of water?

Revision of History: America is not so beautiful any more. At least, not according to some modern history texts. The Gablers note that Patrick Henry's famous line, "Give me liberty or give me death" was left out of forty-three of forty-five history texts reviewed.[9] One fifth-grade history text mentioned George Washington's name only eight times but included seven pages dedicated to Marilyn Monroe.[10] Marilyn who? One book portrayed Benedict Arnold as a hero while another equates Ghandi, John Brown and Martin Luther King with Jesus dying on a cross. In many of the recent history books, America is seen as an imperialistic aggressor nation, a corrupt social quagmire built on selfishness and cutthroat lifestyles. Communism is exalted and globalism is proposed as the answer to the world's problems.

Sex Education: As the Gablers and some staff people were copying some pages from textbooks to take to a hearing, a staff lady finished copying some pages containing some sexually graphic material on which her adult daughter had started working before taking a break. When the daughter returned, she asked her mother why she had finished her task for her. The lady, embarrassed for her daughter, said, "I didn't want you to see the rest of it." "Oh, Mother," the young woman replied, "I had all that stuff when I was in Mrs. Brown's class at school." Mrs. Brown had been her *fourth grade* teacher. " I remember what she told us," the girl went on. "She said, this is part of your school studies that you don't take home. You don't talk about it either, because parents wouldn't understand."[11]

The Gablers quoted school books endorsing homosexuality, bestiality, pre-marital sex and abortion. I was surprised at how graphic the material was and how all consideration of morality was excluded.

Despair Conditioning: The Gablers were impressed with the number of parents calling them to complain about the depressive effect school was having on their children. It soon became evident where the depression came from. Book after book was found that catered to a taste for the sad, the angry, the grim, the violent. Stories in literature books dealt with themes of murder, suicide, rape, gang fights and beatings.

Social psychologist Otto Klineberg compared fifteen American reading primers, including one called *Fun with Our Family*, and concluded that the characters—"gentle and understanding parents, doting grandparents, generous and cooperative neighbors, even warmhearted strangers"—were too *good*. He recommended that frustration, meanness, poverty, and crime be added for balance...

Klineberg wasn't the first or last person to advocate these notions, but his ideas illustrate the crusade to censor from texts the Judeo-Christian virtues of family affection, respect of parents, work, thrift, independence, and achievement.[12]

Besides these mentioned by the Gablers there are still more ungodly themes being programmed into text materials by different special interest groups. At the risk of extending a chapter that is already too long and depressing, let me give a couple of them a brief mention.

Feminism: One way the radical feminists are approaching their crusade to make us a unisex society is by indoctrinating our children through school books. They have put so much pressure on publishing companies that some of the largest ones have issued pamphlets of author guidelines that inform writers that they need not submit books for publication if they do not use sex-neutral terms such as humankind instead of mankind, or congressperson instead of congressman. Pictures given for examples of acceptable text illustrations show fathers nurturing children and women working in factories, etc.

New Age Religion: You may be better informed on this topic than I am, as I haven't yet done much reading on it. It is obvious though, that New Age practices such as channeling, relaxation techniques, spirit guides, etc., are being widely used in schools as well as infiltrating all other institutions of our society. The current strong emphasis on self esteem (often at the expense of challenging academic work) is a popular vehicle for infiltration of New Age doctrine. If you are not familiar as yet with this movement, get informed as I intend to. It comes to us direct from the pit of hell.

I am old enough to remember when school reading books taught lessons of character and moral behavior. Evidently these values have gone the way of the buffalo in most school materials today. Too bad. As William Bennett puts it:

> If we believe that good art, good music and good books will elevate taste and improve the sensibilities of the young—which they certainly do—then we must also believe that bad music, bad art, and bad books will degrade. As a society, as communities, as policymakers, we must come to grips with that truth.[13]

He could have added, as educators.

PART III: DANGER AND OPPORTUNITY

Chapter 8

The Electronic Socializer

It's been called The God With The Glass Face. The average American now sits and stares at it for fifty hours a week, more time than most men spend at their jobs, more time than children go to school, more time than many adults sleep. Almost every home in this country has one, and most have more than one. Its influence is seen in the buying patterns, voting trends and social behavior of the entire nation and much of the world. It is a phenomenon of modern times, unheard of in most households prior to 1950 but today the dominant force in the philosophy of millions. It is television and it is helping to kill America.

I often tell audiences at our seminars that I believe the three greatest threats to our national survival are television, modern music and public education. This is because these

112

three things so deeply influence the way we think in this country, and often influence us not to think at all.

Before you skip this chapter as just another predictable diatribe against the boob tube, relax. I'm not going to start out by throwing a plateful of half-intelligible statistics at you. You've heard all that before—and have you mended your ways? I just want to talk to you for a moment at first as a brother in the Lord and ask you to consider some ideas about TV that I've been mulling over for a long time and that make sense to me.

Often after a workshop or seminar session in which I challenge the addiction of television, some mom or dad will come up to me and say, "We have a television, but we control it." I'm not questioning that there are people who use television without allowing it to enslave them, but I firmly believe that people who watch television and don't waste at least some amount of time and absorb at least some amount of harmful spiritual input are about one in a thousand, if not more rare than that.

For every person who can use television and control it, there are multitudes who cannot. Since our marriage twenty years ago, Marilyn and I have never owned one with the exception of a black-and-white model which was given to us as a monitor for our first computer, also a gift from the same family. We never used it as a source of entertainment and I don't even know it worked for its usual function. I know enough to know that I don't need the temptation of easy entertainment at the touch of a finger.

My first objection to television is that I don't see how anybody can justify the time to watch it. If you have several hours per week to waste, your life must be pretty barren. There are spiritual and physical needs all around us and we have a responsibility as Christians to seek out some of those needs and meet them. It disturbs me that most believers assume that they have the right to decide what to do with their time and spend large chunks of it in an activity that is no activity at all and will yield no worthwhile fruit of any kind. When I think of this assumption it calls to mind an image of a king on a throne, watching the antics of his court jester. He is the ruler of the kingdom and he assumes the right to do with his time what he will. If it accomplishes no more than giving himself a good time, that is perfectly all right. There is of course a sense in which believers are kings, but we are to think of ourselves as servants. We're in this world to meet needs, not to have a good time.

Don't get me wrong. I love to have fun as much as anybody. What I'm saying is that God has priorities for our lives and there is a limit to how much time He wants us to spend in rest and recreation. I won't presume to dictate how many hours per week God has authorized for you. To your own master you stand or fall and I am nobody's master. But I reserve the right to insist that you have a responsibility to analyze it and make an intelligent decision. You are not your own; you are bought with a price. And you can't present your body a living sacrifice and claim for yourself the right to decide what that body will spend its time doing. So I ask you to think it over, make responsible decisions and don't lie to yourself.

Once you've settled the question of how much time is healthy for recreation, the next matter is that of how that time is best spent. I challenge you to find an hour to watch television that couldn't be better spent doing something else. Remember, Christians aren't responsible just to keep from doing harm, but to do as much good with their hours and days as possible, to make the best use of the time God had given us. After all, we don't know how much time we have on this earth, but we do know there is only so much of it.

With this in mind, can you really afford that hour of television? Assuming that what you would watch was absolutely harmless and even educational, is that the best use of the hour? If it's an educational program, could you learn more about the topic from a book? Or, if it's just entertainment, would the hour be better invested playing tennis with your daughter or taking your little boy fishing? You get the point.

A question I often ask folks who strictly limit their viewing is this: Can you get the benefit of that education or recreation without admixture of harmful input? Satan loves to hide a spoonful of poison in a gallon of innocence. And while not all poisons kill instantly, some have a deadly cumulative effect. If your educational show is about science, is there evolution or humanistic philosophy mixed in? If it's an entertainment show, is there any trace of uncleanness or implied contempt for certain persons or groups (or, quite possibly, for God and His standards)? This is not uncommon in comedy shows, for instance.

While you're evaluating all this don't forget that everything you do is an example for your children. We tell our children not that everything on TV is wrong or that everyone who ever watches it is bad, but that it just isn't worth having because so little of it is good and the potential for bad input is so great. We are aware that children use the example of their parents as rationale to do what their parents did, but often more of it. If you are making use of television, do your children really understand the criteria by which you evaluate programming? Or will they someday be a little too casual about what comes through the cable because after all, Mom and Dad used to watch the tube some?

The Socialization Trap

There's an old story about a man who became a Christian and stopped getting drunk on the weekends but would still have a social drink occasionally. One snowy evening, he put on his coat and started down the street for his pub. Something made him look over his shoulder before he had gotten very far and there he saw his little son following him, placing his feet precisely in his father's footprints in the snow to keep his feet dry. Instantly the man was struck by the significance of what his boy was doing and where he would have ended up had he continued to follow those footprints to their intended destination. He turned and walked back to his boy and said, "Come on, son, I was just on my way home." And placing the lad atop his shoulders he made tracks in a better direction.

One of the reasons we don't use alcoholic beverages in our home is that we know that if we never drink, we will never become drunkards. Why expose our family to temptations that are unhelpful and needless? We apply this same logic to television. We don't need it and if we don't have it our children will never acquire a dependence on it.

I spoke recently at the Virginia state home education convention and happened to mention television in my speech. Afterwards a lady came up to me wanting to talk about it. She said she and her family were evidently the one in a thousand who could control television because they watched only a couple of hours per week and only those programs that were educational and of real importance. She was obviously not one of those who come wanting to argue about my puritanical opinions. She wanted to double check and see if I could point out any harm in their very limited viewing. I told her that she and her husband seemed to be exercising responsibility and caution and that I being totally unfamiliar with what is on TV these days, would not attempt to criticize their selections. I did ask her to consider what influences were coming through the screen in the form of commercials.

I once read that advertisers spend more on a thirty-second commercial than is invested in making a thirty-minute program. This means that tremendous amounts of money and the best talent available go into the construction of these commercial messages. Laden with subliminal suggestion, these short promotionals are based on reams of psychological research. That they work is evidenced by the fact that sponsors find it profitable to keep paying incredible sums of money to produce them.

What is the purpose of a commercial? It is to make the viewer want something. It's assumed that the viewer does not already want the product or at least doesn't want it badly enough to go buy it without encouragement. In other words, the idea is to create covetousness in the person watching. And you have only to watch a few commercials to see a wide variety of clever ploys used to create or intensify this desire.Advertisers have learned that sex sells. Attractive, young and scantily clad models are used to sell everything from toothpaste for dental health to soft drinks to rot the teeth. Other commercials use jealousy, social status, fear, self-indulgence and a wide variety of other considerations to sell products that aren't needed to people who would better spend their money otherwise. The net effect of all this is that it is hard if not impossible for Christian families to watch television without opening themselves to a barrage of powerfully suggestive and ungodly thoughts and emotions.hat are some of the products sold on television? Harmful things and useless things along with the good products. Do we really want our children subjected to powerful psychological ploys designed to make them hunger for Barbie, whose role in life seems to be to have it all and be eternally dressed and accoutered in the height of fashion? What are we saying to our children when we allow this into our homes?

> An experimental study by Tan (1979) found that adolescent girls exposed to a heavy dose of beauty commercials were more likely than a control group of girls not exposed to the commercials to believe that being beautiful is an important characteristic and is necessary to attract men. Twenty-three high school girls (16-18 years of age) viewed 15 commercials which emphasized the desirability of sex appeal, beauty, or youth (e.g. ads for toothpaste or soap), and 33 girls viewed commercials which did not contain beauty messages (e.g. ads for dog food, soy sauce, or diapers). They were then asked to rank order the relative importance of ten attributes (e.g. pretty face, intelligence, sex appeal, hard-working, youthful appearance, competence) in each of four areas (career/job, life, to be liked by men, and desirable personal attributes). The beauty ad group ranked the importance of the sex-appeal qualities significantly higher than the neutral ad group for the item "to be liked by men;" marginal significance in the same direction was found for the item "personally desirable." [1]

For the reader who may get the impression that I have never had a television and therefore know nothing of its debits and credits personally, let me interrupt myself for a moment to assure you that TV and I are not unacquainted.

As a matter of fact, I tell my seminar audiences I was reared by a television. That was back in the days before cable brought such a wide variety of garbage into living rooms, but there was little edification in the glowing blue tube even then. But I loved the television and came home from school each day eager for the hours to go by until prime time. I remember the summers in my high school years when my parents were divorced and I stayed home to watch out for my little brother and sister while Mom worked. I would stay up at night watching the late show, then the late, late show and the late, late, late, late, late, almost early show. Then I would sleep until the middle of the next morning and wonder as I stumbled around looking for something for breakfast, how I was going to pass all those hours until the good programs came on again. Remember daytime TV before cable? You see how I suffered.

My television addiction started early. I think I was about six years old when I was lying on the sofa one evening watching the tube and wishing I didn't have the flu. Mom told me not to look at the TV because it would make my headache worse. So I listened and sneaked occasional peeks while my parents and some friends talked over cards in the kitchen. Suddenly the world came to an end: the picture tube went out—and right in the middle of *Tombstone Territory*!

I'll never forget the feeling of desperation that overwhelmed me. I was miserably sick, confined to bed or sofa and that was torture enough for a hyperactive boy. But now my lifeline was severed. The situation was disastrous. Young as I was, I knew that replacing a television was something that took adults some time and that I was facing at least one and perhaps several evenings with no TV. The only answer was to slit my wrists.

But miracles do happen. Someone in the house evidently knew of a used TV set for sale, because that very evening Dad and his friend carried it in, plugged in the cord, connected the lead-in wire and I was saved. I don't recall my dependence on television abating any after that.

This television addiction is certainly not limited to children. I knew a lady whose husband was a professor in a conservative theological seminary. They had not owned a television in years when some friend or relative made them a gift of a nice color set. Well, you can't just throw a gift away, so this man grew addicted to it instead. His relationship with his wife and children deteriorated as he spent in front of the tube, hours which he had once spent available for communication. The crowning inglory was when he chose to eat Thanksgiving dinner in front of the TV instead of at the table with the family. I can't blame this couple's eventual separation exclusively on the television, but it didn't help.

In Marie Winn's book, *Unplugging The Plug-in Drug,* she makes some perceptive observations about television addiction:

> It is in its psychosocial consequences, especially its effects on relationships and family life, that television watching may be as damaging as chemical addiction. We all know the terrible toll alcoholism or drug addiction takes on the families of addicts. Is it possible that television watching has a similarly destructive potential for family life?
>
> Most of us are at least dimly aware of the addictive power of television through our own experiences with the medium: our compulsive

involvement with the tube too often keeps us from talking to each other, from doing things together, from working and learning and getting involved in community affairs. The hours we spend viewing prove to be curiously unfulfilling. We end up feeling depressed, though the program we've been watching was a comedy. And yet we cannot seem to turn the set off, or even not (ital) turn it on in the first place. Doesn't this sound like an addiction?[2]

Much attention has been given to the subject matter on television and I'll have a bit more to say about that later myself, but it should be pointed out that television watching is not only harmful because of what it does to the child, but also what the child is not doing when he is watching.

Every passive hour in front of the tube robs the child of time that might be used to develop other interests and talents, both intellectual and physical. Television opens an international vista to the youngster in the privacy of his home, while denying him time for experiences on his own street corner. Soap opera replaces literature. A spectator's seat on the 50-yard line replaces participatory sports. Unimaginative quiescence replaces creative play. An oration by Big Bird replaces conversation with a parent.[3]

The watching child is not playing, getting healthy exercise. Studies have shown, in fact, that TV tends to make children obese because they sit still for extended periods of time and also increase their junk food intake. Many parents use TV as a baby sitter for this very reason. It has the hypnotic power to keep children quiet and occupied for hours on end. Part of the reason for this is not psychological but physical. Marie Winn quotes research stating that regardless of what is on television at the moment, the watcher's body is going through processes similar to the effects of a mild depressant drug. Electronic Benadryl. This helps to explain why it is so hard to carry on a conversation with a person while he is watching television. Not only is he mentally distracted, he is also in a physical state similar to a mild drug-induced stupor.

The child in front of the television is not communicating. In most cases, he has just spent several hours in a school classroom where he is given only extremely limited opportunity to use words and interpret the verbal responses of others. John Holt pointed out that the people in school who need practice talking are the children but the ones who get it are the teachers. Now the child spends on the average several hours during evenings and weekends absorbing input from the tube instead of communicating with anybody. In fact, the modern American school child has less opportunity to practice communication skills than did his counterpart of a hundred years ago. This is a main reason why television is so effective at stifling social development.

Somebody commented in an article I read years ago that people don't build porches on houses any more. His gist was that we have become less social with our neighbors than we once were. He lamented that the advent of air conditioning and television has drawn us indoors, off the porches and out of the yards, away from the fence on which we used to lean as we gossiped with the people from next door or down the street. The author had a point. And while I thrive on air conditioning, television is something I'd like to see more people do without. Children and adults as well, benefit from the practice of interpersonal communication skills. And while most adults get considerable such practice in the workplace (including women nowadays), the kids are the ones to be left out. While their parents are using real speech on the job or at home, children are confined in desks studying speech but forbidden to use it in its most common forms. Then, home they go to the almighty box.

Children are also not reading while they are in front of the TV. Marilyn and I have found that children will learn to be good readers if they are read to and if the home is supplied with plenty of worthwhile books. However, it's easier to turn on the electronic baby sitter than to go to the library, so many parents opt for the path of least resistance. This robs children of the practice in using written symbols that will be so critical to them all through life. And more opportunity to use humanspeak goes down the—uh,tube (forgive me—couldn't resist).

If your child has a problem with spelling or grammar, it may be because he has spent too much time with his nose in the screen instead of a book. We have found that most of our children haven't needed spelling instruction because they had learned to read phonetically and had seen so many words used in books so many times. They recognize right and wrong spellings when they see them and so have not, as a rule needed to work on lists of "spelling words" or rules. Only a couple of our children have been given spelling assignments at all, thereby freeing us and them to work on more interesting learning. When we do notice a spelling problem, we watch to identify the rule being violated, then assign work relating to that rule rather than giving the child a whole year's worth of spelling instruction.

The Socialization Trap

On the topic of verbal communication, have you noticed that families don't talk much any more? I think it's obvious that a big part of the reason for that is that so many people allow television to dominate their time. On the rare occasions when we have rented a VCR to watch an educational tape or some family shots I have noticed that I have spent an uncomfortable amount of time shushing the younger children so the rest of us could hear. I wonder if the problem isn't intensified when it isn't a tape but a TV program being viewed and can't be rewound and played again.

Another thing a child isn't doing while watching the tube, is thinking. Thinking about serious things for extended periods of time has almost become a lost art in our society. It seems that there is always some racket to keep us distracted and unable to develop a train of thought that ever gets away from the depot. When Americans aren't busy with responsibilities (and sometimes when they are) they are watching television or have a radio playing nearby. The rather obvious result is constant distraction.

We can only speculate as to how much this perpetual preoccupation is costing us. Nobody seems to philosophize 0any more; I wonder how our world would be different if electronic entertainment had always been available. I rather suspect that our society would have been much more shallow and disintegrated a century ago, even as it seems to be now. Would Lincoln, Franklin and Edison, along with other self-educated giants, have ever approached the success for which we now honor them? I have to doubt it.

The main objection heard when conversation turns to television is its programming content. This is the most obvious problem. By and large, the substance of television is mental garbage, spiritual and intellectual rotgut that any thinking person should be ashamed to waste time on.

Some of it is filth and it's pretty obvious to the disinterested observer. But evidently the continuous ingesting of this compost for years desensitizes people, because parents now watch in the presence of their children shows that would have been X-rated at the box office twenty years ago and which they themselves would then have been embarrassed to attend. Very recently I had occasion to be in the home of a stranger and experience a taste of what is on television these days. Every other word was vile profanity. Casual or humorous mention was made of such edifying topics as drunkenness and PMS. I heard a bellyful of garbage and was only in the house less than fifteen minutes.

A less obvious problem is just as prevalent but because of its insidious nature requires more thought to identify. This is the presence of large doses of what Scripture calls vanity. Have you ever watched a game show? I haven't seen more than an odd glimpse of such a program since I was a kid but even then they insulted my intelligence. Hordes of people going ballistic over "fabulous" prizes announced by a host who must have had his training as a sideshow barker. One show features the host calling out the name of the next contestant from the audience who then runs down the aisle and up on stage, grinning, shouting, and waving his hands in wild delight while his colleagues in the crowd scream and cheer in a hopeless attempt to give vent to their uncontrollable joy. Do they really think we're stupid enough to believe all this is genuine? Evidently we are. Such shows stay on the air.

Many of the so-called sitcoms are made of no more substantial stuff. Remember Lucy? She won everybody's hearts by portraying herself as a hopeless imbecile. She was utterly incompetent but we loved her. That was long ago. I don't think you would argue that such entertainment has improved much.

Some of the old shows have been recently been resurrected in the name of "family" entertainment. That means that they have no four-letter words in them. They are considered to be harmless although without intellectual or spiritual nourishment. Rather like eating sterilized cardboard. Wally and Beaver were pretty innocent guys when they weren't in the company of Eddie Haskell, and *Father Knows Best* was about as "squeaky-clean" (note that my poor psyche has been permanently scarred by TV lingo) as one could hope for, but do they really contribute to the development of Christian human beings? After all, every plot involves the creation and resolution of a conflict and nearly all of these conflicts were solved, everybody's needs were met, without any thought of appeal to God. He seemed to be the farthest thing from everybody's minds. Great problems and opportunities arose and were resolved in those programs strictly with human resources (usually in the space of thirty minutes). Is this the view of life we want for our children? The Nelsons were nice folks, but did you ever see Ozzie and Harriet seek an answer to a problem in prayer?

A lot of the old movies have been brought out of mothballs for these "family" programs, too. Having read *The Swiss Family Robinson* as a child, I once accepted the invitation of friends to watch their video of the Disney movie based on the book. What a letdown. This movie, made in the early sixties, was a pale caricature of the story. In Johann Wyss' original book, Father Robinson was a minister who was constantly exhorting his children in Scriptural precepts and leading them in family worship daily. In the Disney version, the only reference to the Lord I recall is a scene on the beach immediately after the family survives the shipwreck and makes it to shore safely. And then Mama Robinson has to remind her husband that thanksgiving is in order.

Unworthy attitudes and values are absorbed by children while watching television, and it's much more subtle than the encroachment of sex and profanity over the years. A prime factor in this process is something whose psychological term I don't know. I guess they'd call it vicarious something or other; I call it identifying with the protagonist.

You've probably noticed that when you're watching television or reading a story in a book you tend to feel some traces of the emotions felt by the leading character in the story. This character, called the protagonist, goes through all sorts of experiences and we go through them with him in our imaginations. This is why when the heroine is climbing the steps in the old haunted mansion where the homicidal maniac is lying in wait with his guillotine we, the watchers grow tense and feel the hair start to rise on the backs of our necks. I recall watching a scary movie on TV when I was small. As the plot thickened I backed off slightly from my usual place on the floor with my nose practically rubbing the screen. Every time the scene grew in tension I'd back up a little more until by the end of the show I was sitting right beside my dad's recliner. Another time, when I was in high school a buddy picked me up and we went to a drive-in movie (remember those?) to watch a horror thriller. The scene was moving toward its terrifying climax and the eerie background music was rising in pitch. I was growing more and more tense, my breathing shallow, my heart pounding. When Kenny reached quietly behind me and tapped me on the far shoulder, I almost had a coronary.

The Socialization Trap

You've recognized the same sort of thing with different emotions in a love scene or felt the excitement of seeing the robbery through the eyes of the robber and scheming how you're going to get away with it. We tend to emotionally put ourselves in the place of the character we're watching. So is all this significant? Yes, it is. Our attitudes are mental structures and the building blocks that comprise them are our individual thoughts. The nutrition experts tell us that physically, "You are what you eat." Spiritually, Scripture says, "you are what you think (Pr.23:7)." We can't fill our minds with a constant flow of emotions that are contrary to godliness and still build godly attitudes. Proverbs 13:20 says, "He who walks with wise men will be wise, but the companion of fools will suffer harm." A friend shared with me his grandmother's version of this admonition: "If you lie down with dogs, you get up with fleas." When we empathize with a television character we are programming his attitudes into our minds.

This business of absorbing the attributes of TV characters is worth thinking about. There's no denying that it happens, because we have all seen many times how children will mimic actions and words of people they have watched on the screen. An eighteen-year-old friend of mine was lying on the sofa one day when his tiny five-year-old brother walked over, seized him by the front of his shirt and growled between his teeth, "Go ahead punk—make my day!"

What kinds of attitudes are available from television? The more obvious ones include violence, sensuality, rebellion and irreverence. But there are other attitudes and values that are less readily apparent.

Although students of mine who are dedicated TV watchers have urged me to modify the following statement, I can find only one fictional character regularly seen on commercial television, Felix Unger of *The Odd Couple*, who is depicted as having an adult's appetite for serious music and whose language suggests that he has, at one time in his life, actually read a book. Indeed, it is quite noticeable that the majority of adults on TV shows are depicted as functionally illiterate, not only in the sense that the content of book learning is absent from what they appear to know but also because of the absence of even the faintest signs of a contemplative habit of mind. (The Odd Couple, now seen only in reruns, ironically offers in Felix Unger not only an example of a literate person but a striking anomaly in his partner, Oscar Madison—a professional writer who is illiterate).[4]

Another phenomenon I've observed has a bearing here. I'm sure there's an impressive psychological term for it, perhaps habituation or acclimation or desensitization. I don't know if any of those technically applies, but let's not worry about it now. It won't be on the exam, anyway. I refer to the fact that we tend to accept as normal, those things which we see happening frequently.

Human beings have a remarkable ability to get used to things. When I graduated from high school in 1970 I couldn't have named anyone among my acquaintances who would have justified abortion. Today we've seen and heard so much about it that the average American has forgotten that unborn babies are still *babies*. The same goes for sex and profanity on television. People think little of a TV movie laden with filthy language because there are tons of them on every day. But if you could transport a citizen of the fifties to the nineties and show him such programming, he would think he had landed in a Swedish bordello. I alluded in an earlier chapter to the fact that we tend to accept age peer social groups as normal. Why is that? It's because we have seen it done that way all our lives. From a Scriptural point of view, age segregation is as weird as birds flying backward but because we see it every day we tend to think of it as normal and natural.

Herein lies another danger of television. On the magic tube we can watch immorality, murder and profanity repeated dozens of times a day. It has ceased to surprise us on television. I believe it has conditioned us to be less surprised by it in real life as well.

Columnist Erma Bombeck commented on this effect of television when she wrote to the networks concerning TV violence:

> She stated that during a single evening she saw twelve people shot, two tortured, one dumped into a swimming pool, two cars explode, a rape, and a man who crawled two blocks with a knife in his stomach. "Do you know something?" she said. "I didn't feel anger or shock or horror or excitement or repugnance. The truth is I didn't feel. Through repeated assaults of one violent act after another, you have taken from me something I valued—something that contributed to my compassion and caring—the instinct to feel."[5]

The letter doesn't name the villain who tied Mrs. Bombeck to her chair and forced her to spend her time watching all this mayhem. There is no doubt, however that there is plenty of mayhem available for those who will submit to it:

> Today there is more brutal violence and explicit sex on television than ever before. It has been estimated that by the time the average child reaches age 18, he will have witnessed more than 15,000 murders on television or in the movies. Research shows that children and even teenagers have a difficult time distinguishing between what is fiction and what is reality. According to researchers, "...heavy exposure to televised violence is one of the causes of aggressive behavior, crime, and violence in society. Television violence affects youngsters of all ages, of both genders, at all socioeconomic levels and all levels of intelligence...It cannot be denied or explained away." In addition, a 1991 survey revealed that only 2 percent of respondents thought that television should have the greatest influence on children's values, but 56 percent believe that it has the greatest influence—more than parents, teachers, and religious leaders combined. [6]

Whether the problem in the programming is violence, immorality, atheism, materialism or simply anti-intellectualism, the constant, repetitive instances of it are sending a clear message to our minds: This is normal, this is real life, this is business as usual.

The electronic idiot box is a fixture of modern society. Such is its hypnotic power that even those who agree that the vast majority of its output is junk cannot usually bring themselves to part with it. Nearly every home in America has at least one, most have more than one and many households have at least one set turned on every waking hour of the day. It would be hard to make a case that television is helping anybody more than it's hurting, but probably the greatest damage is being done to children. Albert Bandura, psychologist at Stanford University, said it well:

> If parents could buy packaged psychological influences to administer in regular doses to their children, I doubt that many would deliberately select Western gunslingers, hopped-up psychopaths, deranged sadists, slap-stick buffoons and the like, unless they entertained rather peculiar ambitions for their growing offspring. Yet such examples of behavior are delivered in quantity, with no direct charge, to millions of households daily.[7]

The social influence of television on children deserves long and serious consideration. Its message of selfishness, vanity, violence, sensuality and the occult are hardly the lessons we want our children to learn about the world around them. Yet, for the average child the elements of that message are driven home daily through clever commercial packaging, endless repetition and dramatic scene and plot strategems designed to teach him to see the world through the eyes of the characters on the screen.

Chapter 9

A Social Circle for Your Family

If you've been depressed by the negative tone of the preceding chapters, cheer up. It will start to get better now as we switch from the negative to the positive side of the socialization question.

I felt it necessary to spend the time on the negative aspects of the issue for a number of reasons. One reason was that most of us are so enamored with the idea that school and the other usual trappings of childhood social life are necessary, that I thought pretty heavy artillery was needed to tear down the false assumptions. Also, I assume many of the home educators who read this book will want to share it with skeptical grandparents, friends, church members and even school officials who worry about social exposure for home taught kids. I wanted to provide them with some substantiation of the fact that school socialization isn't all it's cracked up to be. Still another factor was that while many parents see socialization as a problem in school and elsewhere, they haven't yet put their finger on the elements that they see as damaging to children. I hoped to isolate and articulate for such people some of the specific factors involved.

It's refreshing now to come to this chapter in which we can deal more with what we should be doing and less with what we shouldn't be doing. I may still seem to have less to say on the positive side of things than on the negative. If so, my defense is that social learning, like most truly important learning, comes in the course of doing the "normal" things of life and so doesn't require all the attention that must be given to the remediation of problems that result when we violate natural principles. In this chapter I'd like to point out a few of these natural principles and try to apply them to the creating of a healthy plan for social learning for our children.

Principle #1: SOCIAL LEARNING IS A BYPRODUCT

The most common mistake made by local home education support groups is that they stray from their purpose. Most such groups start out in response to the need of parents (especially moms) for support and encouragement in home education. Parents need to meet to share insights, questions, problems, ideas and resources. But early on, many of them metamorphose into activity groups with the children as the main beneficiaries. The group has moved from providing encouragement for the parents to providing fellowship opportunities for the children.

I recently heard of a local church with its own home education support group which has developed activities for several different age groups of children. That is precisely the opposite of what home education is all about. This group now has activities for the parents that separate them from the kids and age-graded programs that separate the kids from their siblings and other children of other ages. They are far down the road back to Egypt. Why must we confuse activity with productivity? They have just succeeded in once again dividing the family—the most important social group—for the sake of social development.

We learn to have effective relationships with others in the normal processes of living. It does not require all this artificial structuring; in fact such efforts often reproduce the harmful influences that cause many parents to remove their children from school in the first place. It hurts and frustrates me to see unschoolers building these quasi-school systems.

We begin to build a real social environment for our children when we realize that school is an artificial environment unlike any situation in which they will ever again find themselves. Real social learning begins when we set them free from the captivity of artificial social environments and put them back in the real world.

When I say that social learning is a by-product, I mean that it should not be a goal in itself. Obviously, social skills are important. We can't very well get through life without knowing how to communicate, encourage, direct, organize, learn, negotiate, compromise and employ many other people skills. But we need to rethink the process by which we learn these things.

Many of the activities I have attended which were designed for socialization or fellowship were less than effective. Large-group gatherings can be a lot of healthy fun, but usually don't lend themselves well to interpersonal communication. I've experienced much more real fellowship in a gathering of two families than in a support group activity involving twenty families. In-depth conversation takes place much more readily in a setting of calm and privacy than in a gymnasium full of shouting, laughing people.

There is a place for large-group gatherings; I believe in the assembling of the saints for group worship on Sundays, for instance. But the purpose of those meetings is worship, not the development of social skills. The real social interchange takes place in the informal conversations that take place over the pews after the last amen.

Among Christians we use the word fellowship quite often. It's a Biblical term and concept and has been pretty well defined as "two fellows in the same ship." It carries a connotation of comradeship in a cause. Outside my own family, some of the best times of socializing I've experienced were those times when I got together with others to accomplish something that needed to be done in order to meet a need not directly related to socializing.

I recall a work day at church several years ago. It was just the men of the church and so I suppose it would not have met the criteria of some for a legitimate social occasion. But we cleaned and moved and perspired together with plenty of joking and friendly leg-pulling mixed in. When the day was over, I felt closer to the other guys and one or two in particular with whom I hadn't previously been well acquainted. We had gathered to do a job and had accomplished it, but had also enjoyed a church fellowship at the same time. We shared a sense of mission and of accomplishment.

My sons and I have worked on several building projects for Habitat for Humanity. Some of the work we did was through business at reduced prices. Some of the projects we participated in as volunteers. I enjoy these days when I can take the time to get involved because it's an opportunity to do something of a charitable nature, meet some new friends and enjoy a free lunch. Everybody seems to have a good time. And the end result is that somebody gets a good home who did not have one before. I wish somebody would organize such service projects on a strictly Christian basis.

This line of thought leads me to what I might call the model large-group social occasion: the old-time barn raising or house raising. An acquaintance of mine took a drive a few years ago from our town to a festival being held in the Shenandoah Valley area of Virginia. He said that as he was driving along the highway in the very early morning hours, he passed an open field where a group of people were setting up tables on the grass. He wondered what was going on and found out on his way home about sundown. In the formerly empty field dozens of people were sitting at tables eating and behind them stood a barn of which there had been no trace that morning. It was a church group who had gathered to help one of their members put up a barn. The men had brought their tools and the ladies had brought food. The barn was a physical testimony to their care for one another.

On a recent evening, our family was joined for dinner by some friends who are missionaries to China. They have small children, so our younger kids had a good time and we adults had some good conversation between interruptions. To me this is far better socialization than a hectic outing with several other families that is designed for that purpose.

Our intent was to provide a meal for a missionary family, give them some encouragement and answer some parenting questions before their upcoming return to China. Our children got some experience in social relationships which was great, but that wasn't the purpose of the get-together.

It seems to be a standard joke among church people that we can't have fellowship without food. In our church (we happen to be Baptist) I notice that we can't seem to manage without fried chicken in particular. There's always plenty of fried chicken at any of our fellowship gatherings which suits me fine. I love friend chicken and it gives ma a chance to crack my stock joke (the only one I know) that if chickens ever take over the world there will be Kentucky Fried Baptist for sale on every corner.

Seriously, though, there seems to be something to the idea of sharing a meal that has a spiritual aspect. The Lord's Supper is one of the ordinances of the church and has a direct relationship to the idea of unbroken fellowship between a believer and the Lord and other believers. I Corinthians 5:11 instructs us not to eat with an unrepentant sinning believer. The apostle Paul writes in Galatians 2:12 about his rebuke of Peter because of Peter's ceasing to dine with Gentiles after some of his Jewish brethren arrived on the scene. During the Jerusalem revival, in Acts Chapter 2, Scripture tells us that believers were "day by day continuing with one mind in the temple, and breaking bread from house to house, they were taking their meals together with gladness and sincerity of heart, praising God, and having favor with all the people." I've noticed several other instances in Scripture where a shared meal was associated with fellowship and hospitality.

In the days of the Old West there were certain Indian tribes who considered it a binding act of friendship to eat a meal with someone. For this reason, trappers and traders were always eager to dine with these people because it made travel in the region much safer.

I'm not sure just what it is about group dining that tends to cement people together but there seems to be something to it. Someday somebody will do a complicated scientific study and find out that during eating the body produces chemicals that make the brain feel friendly or something. That will be fine, but for now we can take advantage of the phenomenon of gastric socialization without fully understanding it. Let's eat.

Principle #2: # THE FAMILY IS A SOCIAL GROUP

It's interesting that when the conversation among home educators turns to socialization nobody talks about the family much. We seem to assume that social learning takes place anywhere but at home. This assumption is not shared by social scientists. In our society, the preponderance of research on social attitudes of children starts with the influence of parents on their children. It's only in recent years that researchers have seemed to wake up to the fact that children are increasingly separated and alienated from their moms and dads. Now more attention is being given to the social effects of school and other influences.

As recently as the 1960's, however, Americans still seemed to look to the family as the source of social attitudes:

> The prevailing view in American society—indeed, in the West generally—has held that the child's psychological development, to the

extent that it is susceptible to environmental influence, is determined almost entirely by his parents, and within the first six years of life at that. And scientific investigators—who are, of course, also products of their own culture, imbued with its tacit assumptions about human nature—have acted accordingly. Western studies of influences on personality development in childhood overwhelmingly take the form of research on parent-child relations, with the peer group, or other extraparental influences, scarcely being considered.

In other cultures, this is not always so. A few years ago, at the International Congress of Psychology held in Moscow, the author was privileged to chair a symposium on: "Social Factors in Personality development." Of the score of papers presented at the symposium, about half were from the West (mostly American) and half were from the socialist countries (mostly Russian). Virtually without exception the Western reports dealt with parent-child relationships, while those from the Soviet Union and other East European countries focused equally exclusively on the influence of the peer group, that is, the children's collective.[1]

Home is, in fact, the best place in the world to learn about living successfully with other people. It is, of course, the scene of nearly all our early interpersonal experiences except in the case of day-care infants, victims of the new American tragedy. It will be a generation or two before we can really judge just how much damage this early separation from parents is doing, but the resulting alienation is not hard to see. One young mother at a gathering of parents and children commented:

> One little girl stood out because of her big blue eyes and blonde hair (I always thought "my" little girl would look like that). Becoming acquainted with her mother, I found that she worked from 8:00 AM to 5:00 PM five days a week. "Boy, I'll bet you really miss her!" I said. "Oh, no," she replied. Noticing how surprised I looked, she explained, "You see, I went right back to work three weeks after she was born, so I never really got used to being with her long enough to miss her now." [2]

As children are being separated from their parents at ever earlier ages, the "generation gap" that once was thought to exist only between parents and teenagers is creeping downward on the age scale.

> Because of the exposure of many very young children to early out-of-home care, the shift from parental to peer dependence may be well developed by the preschool level. A generation ago, this was noticeable only among teenagers. Unfortunately, since their young peers are generally not carriers of sound ethical values, the children learn bad habits and manners, but not the difference of right from wrong, the reason for rules, or the value of work. As we have emphasized, until the age range of about eight to twelve, children are not consistently reasonable.[3]

Two investigations in the nineteen-fifties indicated that, in the age range studied (twelve to eighteen years), although both sources were influential, the peer group tended to outweigh parents in influencing children's values and acts. A broader perspective is provided by the first...comprehensive research on this question carried out by two sociologists...in 1959. Working with a sample of several hundred students from the fourth to the tenth grades in the Seattle school system, these investigators studied age trends in the tendency of children to turn to parents or to peers for opinion, advice, or company in various activities. In general, there was a turning point about the seventh grade. Before that, the majority looked mainly to their parents as models, companions, and guides to behavior; thereafter, the children's peers had equal or greater influence.

Recently, Condry and Simon completed a study designed to reveal current trends in the reliance of children on parents versus peers as sources of information and opinion. The results show a substantially greater percentage of peer "dependence" at every age and grade level than did Bowerman's and Kinch's study. It would appear that the shift from parents to peers as the child's major source of information occurs at an earlier time than it did a decade ago and is now much more pronounced. [4]

The Socialization Trap

I was interested to note here that the seventh grade was found to be a point at which children seemed to shift from trusting their parents for influence to trusting peers. Yet this is the very age at which many home educators put their children in school to "be with kids their own age." Maybe this is just a smoke screen. It is also around junior high school age that children often become more of a challenge to their parents, as they mature to the point of understanding that their moms and dads are not really omniscient. These years can be a trying time and I wouldn't be surprised if many parents are tempted to give up on home education and use the supposedly helpful social opportunities of school as an excuse. And there are some parents who home educate through elementary school age but don't feel confident to teach their children the higher levels of material. Whatever the reason, I think the above mentioned research should give us all food for thought. Kids are under more pressure now than ever before and to put them into the pressure cooker of school society just at a time when their minds are turning a page and their hormones are going crazy, cannot be other than asking for trouble.

The point of all this discussion on the family as a social group is this: Don't sell your birthright for a mess of pottage. The most important things your child ever learns about living with people will be the things he learns at home. The twenty-four-hours-a-day classroom of the family cannot be beaten for a social training camp. The most important, most intense, and most educational human relationships are those formed and fostered in the family. They are the foundation upon which the individual's godly adjustment to his society rests.

Conclusion

In a nutshell, the message of this book has been that God's natural and Biblical way of learning to live with others is better than man's way. Man talks about socialization, God talks about companionship.

As I have attempted to explain in the previous pages, I felt that I needed to take a negative slant in *The Socialization Trap* because of the prevalent tendency among home educators to rebuild for home taught students, the same damaging, age peer-oriented social environment they had escaped by staying out of school. I've been assisted in clarifying and developing my views for this revised edition, by a number of readers who were kind enough to write me and share their thoughts on the subject. Some complimented me on my work and others criticized me, but all contributed to my learning process. They have my thanks.

But the job is far from finished. *The Socialization Trap* was an attempt to deal with the immediate problem by telling people what *not* to do. The next step is to discern from Scripture what we *should* do in regard to training our children to live in a world full of people. There are, no doubt, many people more qualified than I, to write a book of that nature. If, however, such a book doesn't appear before the Lord enables me to have the time to attempt it myself, I will count on my readers to once again grant me the assistance of their input.

If the effort of writing and revising *The Socialization Trap* results in freedom from peer pressure for even one family, it will have been well worthwhile. It isn't easy to swim against the current, but the easy road to travel leads downhill. If America is to see a revival, parents must learn to seek God's way instead of following the crowd. Going with the flow means producing more masses of confused, insecure, purposeless young adults. Seeking God's way means discipling a generation of champions for the King's service.

MATERIALS AVAILABLE from
The Boyers

BOOKS

Home Educating With Confidence   Paperback **$10.95**

When Rick and Marilyn Boyer started home educating the eldest of their four children a decade and a half ago, they didn't know what they were getting into. Fifteen years and eight additional children later, they know exacly what they got into—and they love it! Learn from their experience and find out how you, too can experience the adventure of **Home Educating** *with Confidence!*

Yes, They're All Ours   Paperback **$9.95**

The story of the Boyer family—what life is like in a family of fourteen and why they have chosen to live that way. Some chapter titles: Why So Many?—How Can You Afford It?—How We Got to Be Us—Getting It All Done—And You Home School, Too?—On Having It All Together—Savor the Season—Doesn't Everybody Have Twelve Children?

Written with warmth and humor, *Yes, They're All Ours* contains the special feature, "Family Snapshots:" Pages of hilarious family anecdotes interspersed between chapters.

The Socialization Trap   Paperback **$7.95**

Most home educators reject school for their children partly because of the damage done to them by the pressures of the age peer social group. Yet many parents try to replace lost "social contact" by placing their children in a variety of age-graded activities that recreate the peer pressure all over again. This book tells why you don't need to! The answer you need to the constant question: "What about socialization?"

Fun Projects for Hands-On Character Building
Softcover **$7.95**
This book contains the Boyers' philosophy of spiritual training in a nutshell. Scores of simple, enjoyable projects for parents and children together. Chapters: Building Obedience – Building a Pure Heart – Building a Hunger for Righteousness – Building a Forgiving Spirit – Building Meekness – Building a Strong Testimony.

The Hands-On Dad   *Softcover* **$9.95**
In *The Hands-On Dad,* Rick shares seven Biblical functions for the father and shows how they apply in home education. These important and practical insights can set both Mom and Dad free to be their best for their children.

Proverbs People Workbook 1   *Spiral Bound* **$10.95**
A big workbook chock-full of short-answer questions, example stories, fun quizzes, application questions, and coloring pages teaching the character types in Proverbs. Book 1 teaches the following characters: "Slothful/Diligent"; "Righteous/Wicked"; "The Five Fools"; "The Prudent Man"; "The Wise Man"; "Liar/Faithful Witness". Recommended for ages 8-12.

Proverbs People, Book 2   *Spiral Bound* **$10.95**
Teaches the following character types: "Virtuous Woman vs. Contentious Woman"; "Talebearer"; "Proud vs. Humble"; "Fearful vs. Trusting"; "Angry Man vs. Patient Man"; "Content vs. Covetous"; "Cruel vs. Merciful"; "Flatterer vs.

Honest". Includes short-answer questions, example stories, fun quizzes, application questions, and coloring pages. It's just like Proverbs Vol. I, but with new topics!

Uncle Rick Reads the Proverbs   **$15.00**
A five-hour cassette series. Rick Boyer reads the book of Proverbs just as he reads it to his own kids – complete with comments, colorful example stories and simple explanations of unusual words in the text. If your child doesn't like nap time, let Uncle Rick read him to sleep!

Proverbs Memory Tapes   **$8.00**
The entire book of Proverbs on two sixty-minute cassettes. Play this for your children at nap time and bed time. You'll be amazed at how quickly even the very little ones begin to memorize the simple truths of this great book!

The Runt   **$10.00**
An adventure novel on tape for young people: God uses a hound puppy to teach a boy an important lesson about life.

Uncle Rick Reads His Favorite Psalms   **$12.00**
Selected Psalms read for children with comments and character lessons.

Uncle Rick Reads the Gospel of Matthew   **$10.00**
The Gospel of Matthew read for children, with clarifying comments to help them internalize the Scriptures.

Uncle Rick Tells Bible Stories, Volume I   **$8.00**
Creation through the flood.
Uncle Rick Tells Bible Stories, Volume II   **$8.00**
Tower of Babel through Isaac.
Uncle Rick draws character lessons from these wonderful old stories in Scripture.

OTHER PRODUCTS

Proverbs Flash Cards   **$4.50**
They're simple, they're plain, and *they work*. When you see
how much fun your children have memorizing the Proverbs
verses on these cards, you'll wonder why you didn't think of
making them yourself. 31 cards per set, with illustrations to
color. Recommended for children ages 3-8.

NEW!!! "If and When..." Flash Card Set   **$4.00**
Flash cards feature a question and Scripture reference on one
side, and the answer – the actual verse – on the other side.
For example: "When tempted to hate correction: Proverbs
12:1." Flip the card over and read, "Whoever loves discipline
loves knowledge, but he who hates reproof is stupid."

NEW!!! Character Quality Flash Card Set   **$4.00**
Flash cards feature a question and picture to color on front
side, and verse and reference on the other. For example:
"Why should we choose Godly friends?" Other side: "He who
walks with wise men shall be wise. But the companion of
fools suffers harm." Proverbs 13:20

NEW!!! The Hands-On Dad   **$10.00**
Book on tape, read by Rick Boyer.

SINGLE CASSETTES   **$4.00 each**
Dad: Leader in the Home *(the father's role in home
      education)*
Socialization: All is Not Good
Raising Cain – and Abel
Proverbs: God's Character Curriculum
Home Educating with Confidence
Careers Without College

To order:

For books, include 10% postage and handling, minimum $2.50. For single cassettes, include $1.50 postage and handling. If outside the U.S., enclose 15% (minimum $5.00) in U.S. funds.

Make checks payable to:

The Learning Parent
2430 Sunnymeade Rd.
Rustburg, VA 24588

NOTES

Chapter Two

1. William J. Bennett, *Index of Leading Cultural Indicators*, (The Heritage Foundation 1993) p. i

2. Bronwyn Davies, *Life in the Classroom and Playground*, (Routledge and Kegan Paul 1982) p. 68

Chapter Three

1. Diane E. Papalia and Sally Wendkos Olds, *A Child's World*, (McGraw-Hill 1986), pp. 423,424

2. Ibid., p.424

3. Ibid., p.425

4. Ibid., p.423

5. John Holt, *Teach Your Own*, (Delacorte Press/Seymour Lawrence 1981) pp. 48,49

6. Ibid., p. 49

7. John Taylor Gatto, *Dumbing Us Down*, (New Society Publishers 1992) p.31

8. Urie Bronfenbrenner, *Two Worlds of Childhood*,

(Simon and Schuster)

9.   Gordon, *Home Schools*, p. 20

10.   Bronfenbrenner pp. 101,102

11.   Gatto p. 30

Chapter Four
1.   James Marshall, *The Devil in the   Classroom,*
      (Schocken Books) p.15

2.   John Holt, *Teach Your Own*, (Delacorte
      Press/Seymour Lawrence 1981) p.47

3.   Marshall p. 105

4.   William J. Bennett   The *Devaluing of
      America* (Summit Books 1992) p.75

5.   Marshall p. 46

Chapter Five
1.   Diane E. Papalia and Sally Wendkos Olds, *A
      Child's World*, (McGraw-Hill 1986) p. 408

2.   Urie Bronfenbrenner, *Two Worlds of Childhood*,
      (Simon and Schuster, 1970) p.138

3.   James Marshall, *The Devil in the Classroom*,
      (Schocken Books) p. 34

4.   John Holt, *Teach Your Own*, (Delacorte
      Press/Seyour Lawrence, 1981) p.39

5.   John Taylor Gatto, *Dumbing Us Down*, (New Society Publishers,1992) pp. 47-50

Chapter Six

1.   John Holt, *Teach Your Own*, (Delacorte Press/Seymour Lawrence,1981) pp. 48,49

2.   Ibid., pp.49,50

Chapter Seven

1.   Samuel Blumenfeld, *NEA: Trojan Horse in American Education*, (Paradigm Co., 1984)

2.   William J. Bennett, *The Devaluing of America*, p.205

3.   Mel and Norma Gabler, *What Are They Teaching Our Children?*, (SP Publications, 1985) pp. 31,32

4.   Kathleen M. Gow, *Yes, Virginia, There Is Right And Wrong* , (Tyndale House Publishers, 1985) p. 40

5.   Ibid., p. 162

6.   Ibid., pp. 114-118

7.   Gabler, p. 44

8.   Ibid., p. 41

9.   Ibid., p. 48

10.   Ibid., p. 47

11.   Ibid., pp. 65,66

12.   Ibid., p.92

13.   Bennett, p. 33

Chapter Eight

1.   Robert M. Liebert, Joyce N. Sprafkin and Emily S.
      Davidson, *The Early Window*, (Pergamon Press,
      1982), p.98

2.   Marie Winn, *Unplugging the Plug-in Drug*,
      (Penguin Books, 1987), p. 16

3.   Gene Maeroff, *Don't Blame the Kids*, (McGraw-
      Hill, 1982), p. 32

4.   Neil Postman, *The Disappearance of Childhood*,
      (Delacorte Press, 1982), p. 27

5.   Pamela Tuchsherer, *TV Interactive Toys, The New
      High Tech Threat to Children*, (Pinaroo Publishing,
      1988), p. 49

6.   William J. Bennett, *Index of Leading Cultural
      Indicators*, (The Heritage Foundation, 1993), p.
      20

7.   Robert M. Liebert, Joyce N. Sprafkin and Emily S.
      Davidson, *The Early Window*, (Pergamon Press,
      1982), p. 8

Chapter Nine

1. Urie Bronfenbrenner, *Two Worlds of Childhood*, (Simon and Schuster, 1970), pp.103,104

2. Paul D. Meier and Linda Burnett, *The Unwanted Generation*, (Baker Book House, 1980), p. 24

3. Raymond and Dorothy Moore, *Home Style Teaching*, (Word Books, 1984), p.157

4. Urie Bronfenbrenner, *Two Worlds of Childhood*, (Simon and Schuster, 1970), p.105